Cambridge English Readers

Level 5

Series editor: Philip Prowse

The Sugar Glider

Rod Neilsen

CAMBRIDGE
UNIVERSITY PRESS

CAMBRIDGE
UNIVERSITY PRESS

University Printing House, Cambridge CB2 8BS, United Kingdom

One Liberty Plaza, 20th Floor, New York, NY 10006, USA

477 Williamstown Road, Port Melbourne, VIC 3207, Australia

314–321, 3rd Floor, Plot 3, Splendor Forum, Jasola District Centre, New Delhi – 110025, India

79 Anson Road, #06–04/06, Singapore 079906

Cambridge University Press is part of the University of Cambridge.

It furthers the University's mission by disseminating knowledge in the pursuit of education, learning and research at the highest international levels of excellence.

www.cambridge.org
Information on this title: www.cambridge.org/9780521536615

First published 2003

Printed in Great Britain by Ashford Colour Press Ltd.

A catalogue record for this publication is available from the British Library

ISBN 978-0-521-53661-5 Paperback

Contents

Characters

Don Radcliffe: a pilot
Judy Radcliffe: Don's daughter
Sylvia: Don's ex-wife
Paul Copeman: a pilot
Beulah Copeman: Paul's wife
Patrick Forsha: a businessman
John Fittock: a sheep farmer
Joe: a Murri boy
Berjenka: a foreign businessman
Carl Petersen
Noel Hogan: a government agent

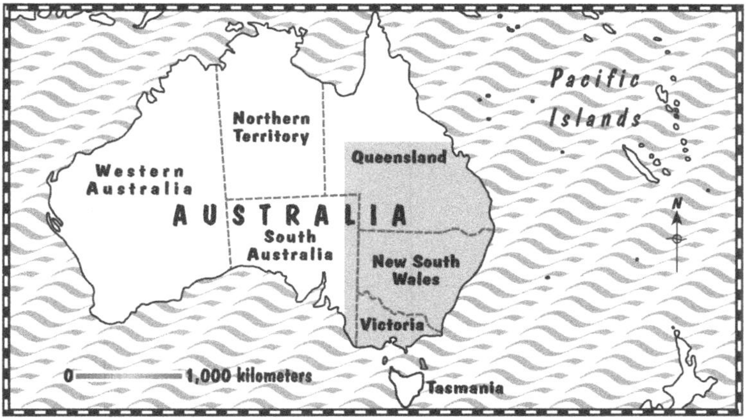
Pacific Islands
Northern Territory
Queensland
Western Australia
AUSTRALIA
South Australia
New South Wales
Victoria
0 1,000 kilometers
Tasmania
N

Queensland
Warrangi mine
Sylvia and Judy's farm
Everett's Field
Brisbane
Gold Coast
Tarong station
Crash spot
New South Wales
Sydney
N
Canberra
Victoria
Melbourne
0 500 kilometers

Prologue

The boat came to a stop. A man in a blue shirt shouted 'South Bank' and opened a gate in the side of the boat. The passengers began walking off the boat, into the beautiful park in the heart of the city.

Among the passengers was a man in his late fifties with white hair and a red face. He walked slowly, breathing a little heavily. He went across the grass to the Café Marcos and sat down at one of the tables outside, facing the river. On the opposite bank he could see the tall modern buildings of the city centre. It was a bright Saturday afternoon in November, a typical late spring day in Brisbane, Australia. There was a cool wind.

He looked at his watch: two o'clock, the time he had agreed to meet a man he didn't know. He looked around. There was a play area nearby, full of children. Groups of families were walking on the path next to the river. He heard a voice behind him.

'I'm Petersen.' A tall, thin man of about thirty-five, wearing dark glasses, was standing by the table. He pulled out a chair and sat down. Then he took a mobile phone and a notebook from his pocket and put them on the table.

'It's a lovely afternoon,' said the white-haired man. 'A good day for flying.'

'I haven't got much time, Mr Copeman. Let's get on with business,' Petersen replied.

Copeman looked at him closely. 'You told me on the phone you had a job for me. Who are you?'

'I work for the government. We know you're a good pilot. We need you to fly to a mine out west to pick up some equipment and chemicals. It's quite simple, but the job needs to be kept secret.'

'Why?' Copeman asked.

'The mine is in the news at the moment. The area has a special meaning for the first Australians, the Murri people in particular, and they're demonstrating to get their land back.' The man picked up his notebook and wrote some numbers down.

'I'm busy. I've got a job flying to Melbourne,' Copeman said.

'We know about that,' Petersen interrupted. 'You're flying an old plane from Brisbane to the Melbourne Air Museum.' Copeman was surprised. How did Petersen know? Petersen continued: 'The timing is perfect for our job. You can land at the mine, pick up what we need and continue your journey to Melbourne. It'll only take a few extra hours, and you'll be well paid for your trouble.'

He pushed the notebook across the table. Copeman looked in amazement at the numbers written there.

'That's a lot of money, I think you'll agree,' said Petersen. 'It would be a big help towards the cost of your new flying school.'

'How do you know so much about me?' Copeman asked.

'That's our business. We know that you want to retire from long-distance flying and start a flying school.'

Copeman thought to himself. With that amount of money, he could start the school soon.

'There's something else,' Petersen said, and wrote again in his notebook. 'You'll need a good co-pilot with you.'

'I don't know if I can find anyone that quickly.'

'Yes, you can.' Petersen put his notebook on the table, next to Copeman and pointed to a name. 'This is a friend of yours, isn't it?'

Another surprise. 'He's not even in Australia at the moment' Copeman replied. 'He's been working in the Pacific Islands . . . '

'We know he's coming back next week, and we know you're meeting him. He's an experienced pilot. We know you could both do a good job for us.'

'And where should we take the stuff that we pick up?' Copeman asked.

'Don't worry about that,' Petersen replied. 'Just fly on to Melbourne as you planned – we'll arrange the rest.' A small smile moved across his face. 'So, what's your answer? Yes or no? We need to know now.'

Copeman looked towards the river. Another boat was coming in. He thought hard. It was a lot of money, and he thought he could persuade his friend. Most pilots loved the romance of flying older planes. And there was another thing. His friend had gone off to the Pacific Islands last year after an unhappy divorce and left his family behind. If they could start the flying school together, his friend could stay in Australia and perhaps he could get his family back together again. Family was the most important thing. Copeman looked at the children over in the playground. He had no children himself.

'All right,' he whispered.

Petersen picked up his mobile phone and rang a

number. When someone answered, he got up and walked a little way from the table. 'He says yes, Mr F,' Copeman heard Petersen say. Then Petersen put the phone back in his pocket and pulled out two envelopes. The first one had nothing written on it.

'This is all the information you need about where and when to go,' Petersen said and handed the envelope to Copeman. On the front of the second envelope it said simply: N. Manderville, Manager, Warrangi Mine.

'When you get to the mine, give this to the manager.' Petersen handed the second envelope to Copeman. 'Oh, and there's one last thing.'

'What?' Copeman asked.

'Make two flight plans, one to Melbourne direct and one stopping at Warrangi, but that's just for you. Hand in the first one to the airfield office, and destroy the other one when you've finished using it. No one except you and the co-pilot must know you're stopping at Warrangi.'

Copeman was not sure. 'But it's against the law . . .'

'It's for your government, remember? Just make sure nothing goes wrong.' Petersen got up. 'We'll put half the money in your bank while you're away. You'll get the rest when the job is done,' said Petersen. Then he left.

Chapter 1 *Coming home*

Don Radcliffe looked ahead from the window of his new aeroplane. It was small, a two-seater. He had been flying for hours, with nothing but the blue Pacific Ocean beneath him. Now he could see a green line coming towards him. It was the east coast of Australia. Home. Or was it? He wasn't sure any more. Perhaps his real home was up here, high above the earth.

It was a year since he'd seen Australia; a year of jobs flying around the beautiful islands of the Pacific; a year since his divorce. He'd saved enough to buy this small plane, and had money left over. Then his old friend and teacher Paul Copeman had called him. Paul wanted to retire and start a flying school. Why didn't Don come back and join him, Paul had asked. Don knew it wasn't just for the business. Paul and his wife Beulah had been upset about Don's divorce. He had always been like a son to the older couple, and it had hurt them to see Don leave his wife Sylvia and his teenage daughter Judy. It had hurt Don too, but at the time he had just wanted to get away. Now he was coming back and soon he would see them all again.

At last he could see Brisbane below him. Its river went through the heart of the city like a silver snake. He turned the plane southeast, following the river, flying over the green suburbs. In a few minutes he could see Everett's Field, a small airfield, used mostly by private planes. There were a number of small planes on the ground. He moved the controls and the plane began to go down.

As the airfield came closer, he noticed a large silver-grey plane in a corner of the field. 'That looks like an old Douglas DC4, from the Second World War,' Don thought. 'There aren't many of those left. I wonder what it's doing here.'

Like most pilots, he loved all types of planes, especially old ones. They were simpler, and more fun to fly.

He circled the airfield, looking for Sylvia's Land Cruiser. There were a few cars near the office buildings, but none of them was Sylvia's. 'Had she got a new car since he went away?' he wondered.

Sylvia had been surprised when he'd called her the week before, but she'd promised to bring Judy, their daughter, to meet him. Judy was fourteen now, and Don was missing her growing up. Judy and Don were planning to stay with the Copemans for a few days. Don had promised to take Judy for trips in his new plane. Sylvia had sounded happy with the idea, and Judy had been very excited.

Don hoped he could see more of Sylvia too and he hoped that Sylvia felt the same. He was sorry things had got so bad between them. The stress of a pilot's life had been difficult for them both. He had been away from home a lot, and Sylvia had never liked it. Perhaps a year was long enough to forget the past.

He felt the wheels of the plane touch the ground. He braked and after slowing down. The plane finally came to a stop. Taking a case from behind the pilot's seat he climbed out and looked around. A few mechanics were servicing some of the planes. He walked towards the airfield buildings. Over near the fence, a man with white hair was waving. Don called out, 'Hey, Paul!'

'Hello, Don! How's it going? Is that your new plane? She looks good.'

Don reached the fence. 'She's beautiful to fly. She almost flies herself. We'll have to take her up together, Paul. It's good to see you!' They shook hands warmly.

'I was expecting to see Sylvia and Judy here too. Haven't they arrived?' Don asked.

Paul shook his head. 'Not yet. I'm looking forward to seeing them again, though. I haven't seen them since they moved out to the farm. I've missed you all, Don.'

'I suppose they'll be here soon. Let's go into the office. I have to check in my papers.' As they walked towards the office, the old plane across the airfield caught Don's eye. It was shining in the sun. He stopped for a moment.

'By the way, Paul,' he said, 'I noticed that old plane as I was coming in. It's a DC4, isn't it?'

'That's the *Sugar Glider*.' Paul smiled.

'Is it still flying?'

'Not for much longer. It's been sold to a museum. Why, would you like to fly it?' Paul asked.

'Sure, I love those old planes . . .' Don saw the expression on Paul's face. 'You're serious, aren't you?'

'Yes, I am serious. A job has come up, Don, and I need your help.'

'Tell me about it,' Don said.

'I want you to help me fly that DC4 to Melbourne. Tomorrow. How about it?'

'Tomorrow?' Don laughed.

'That's right.'

Don looked at his friend for a moment. 'Paul, you know I promised to spend some time with Judy. It's been a year, remember? I haven't been a very good father.'

'I understand, Don, but it wouldn't take much time.'

'Why do you need me? You can fly it by yourself, can't you?'

Paul thought for a moment. He didn't want to tell Don how Petersen had insisted on Don flying with him. Not yet.

'I just thought you might be interested. There aren't too many of those planes left.'

'What is the job, exactly?' Don was curious.

Paul smiled. 'It's going to the Melbourne Air Museum – its last flight – but I also have to make a stop on the way, at a mine out west, and pick some things up for the government. That mine is in the middle of nowhere. Really, I could use some help.'

Don noticed Paul was breathing quite fast. 'Are you OK, Paul?' he asked, putting a hand on his friend's shoulder.

'I'm fine, Don. Don't worry.'

'OK. So it's just a trip to Melbourne?'

'Sure. The whole trip will only take two days, and they're paying a lot of money. We could use it for the flying school.'

'I don't know, Paul. What about Judy?' Don said.

'I know, I know. I want you to be with her too, but there'll be plenty of time, now you're back. There aren't many chances to fly planes like this one, Don. You know you'd love it. Two days, I promise. Judy can stay at the house with Beulah. She'll like that.'

'Just two days?' Don said.

'Sure. The mine's only a couple of hours away. It's a place called Warrangi. We'll pick up some chemicals and equipment, then go straight down to Melbourne. We'll stay overnight, look at the museum, and maybe go to one of those nice Greek restaurants in the city. I've even got return flights reserved.'

Don grinned. 'Were you so sure I'd do it?'

'Two days, Don,' Paul said. 'Then you can take Judy wherever you want!'

Don thought it over. He was looking forward to spending time with his daughter, but it was true, there would be plenty of time later. He intended to stay in Australia if the flying school worked out. Sylvia would be angry, of course. She had always complained that his love of flying came before his family. But it was his job, and he loved it. And when would he get another chance like this?

'I suppose it'll be OK,' he said at last.

'Good man!' Paul smiled.

Chapter 2 *A family meeting*

Two hours later, Paul and Don were still sitting in the office, drinking coffee and talking about Don's work in the Pacific Islands. From the window Don saw a red Land Cruiser coming up the narrow airfield road towards them. It came to a stop near the office and a woman got out. Don got up, his heart beating fast as he recognised Sylvia. She looked nervous. Then Judy got out too. She was taller than Don remembered her, but she still had her long dark wavy hair, tied back as always, and the same pretty face as her mother. She looked brown and well from her outdoor life in the country, Don thought. Don and Paul went outside to meet them.

'Hello, Judy,' Don said, going forward to kiss her. She bent her face towards him and smiled. 'Hi, Dad,' she said. 'Welcome home.'

'Who is this lovely young woman?' said Paul. Judy smiled and put her arms round him. Paul had always been like a favourite uncle to her.

'Where's your new plane?' Judy asked her father.

Don pointed across the airfield. 'Can you see that two-seater with the red line down the side?'

'Yes. It looks cool.'

'That's it,' he said.

'When can we go up in it? Tomorrow?'

'Soon. We'll talk about it later.' Don said, looking at the ground.

Sylvia came towards them. 'Hi', she said nervously. She kissed Don quickly on the cheek, then turned to Paul. 'It's wonderful to see you,' she said.

'Nice to see you again, Sylvia,' said Paul. 'How are things down on the farm?'

'Good thanks, Paul.'

'We were worried about you,' Don said.

'Look, I'm really sorry we're so late. There was a lot of traffic on the roads because there are demonstrations this week out west.'

'Demonstrations?' Don had not followed the news in his home country for some time.

'It's about land rights for people like the Murri,' said Judy excitedly. 'We've been studying it in school.'

'Have you?' said Don. 'So you know all about it?'

'Yes,' said Judy, and gave him a history and politics lesson right there on the airfield. Don smiled proudly. He knew, of course, about how the British in the nineteenth century had started building cities and farms on the Murri people's lands – lands they had previously wandered for 40,000 years. But he was out of touch with the progress the Murri people were making in fighting back.

'So now they want some of it back, at least some of the special places. They should have some rights, shouldn't they?' Judy finished.

'I suppose they should,' Don said. 'You'll have to tell me more about it later.'

Paul decided it was time to leave Don alone with his family. 'Don, I have to check a few things. When you're ready we'll take Judy back to my place. Are you coming too, Sylvia?'

'No, not today, Paul. I have to go into the city.' She was looking around as if expecting someone. 'I'll see you and Beulah again soon, I'm sure.'

'OK. Take care then,' Paul said and walked back into the office.

'I'll catch up with you in a few minutes,' Don said. There was a long silence when Paul had gone.

'So, how are the Pacific Islands?' Sylvia said at last.

'It's a beautiful part of the world,' Don replied.

'Yes, I know you were happy there,' said Sylvia.

'And how's the farm?' Don asked.

'It's good. I'm glad I kept it after my parents died. It's a nice change, although I miss the city sometimes. It's such a long drive. It's been good for Judy though. She really likes it now.'

'Is that right, Judy?' Don looked at his daughter.

'Sure. I'm learning all sorts of stuff about living in the bush and I ride my horse everywhere.'

'So you have a horse now? How long have you been riding?' Don asked.

'About four months,' Judy answered.

'She can ride very well,' Sylvia said, not meeting Don's eye.

'So you're going into the city?' Don asked. 'I was thinking, maybe we could all have dinner.'

Sylvia shook her head. 'Not today. I'm . . . I'm meeting a friend.'

She changed the subject. 'It will be nice for Judy to fly with you. She's looking forward to it so much. Look, I'm really sorry we were so late. I expect you want to take her back to Paul's soon.'

'There's no hurry,' said Don. 'Not for me,' he thought, but Sylvia seemed anxious for him to leave.

At that moment, they heard the noise of an engine above them and looked up. A helicopter was coming towards the airfield.

'I hope I can visit the farm,' Don continued. 'I may be here for a while, if we start this flying school . . .'

He realised Sylvia wasn't listening. She was looking at the helicopter, which was landing a hundred meters away. The engine stopped, and Don saw a tall man with shiny black hair get out of the pilot's seat. He was wearing a light business suit. He came towards them, waving. Sylvia's face went red.

'What's he doing here?' said Judy.

'Hello Sylvia, hello Judy,' said the man as he reached them. 'And you must be Don. Sylvia told me she was meeting you here. Welcome back to Australia.'

'Don, this is Patrick Forsha,' said Sylvia in a small voice.

They shook hands. 'We've met, but you probably don't remember, Don. At a party a couple of years ago,' Patrick said.

'Maybe, I'm not sure.' Don thought back. He thought he remembered Patrick's face. He looked like the sort of rich businessman who liked to show he had money. What was he doing here? He noticed that Patrick smiled at him with his mouth, but not with his eyes.

'And how's that horse I bought you?' Patrick said to Judy. 'Your mother tells me you're an expert rider now.'

'Her name's Sasha,' Judy said, rather coldly, Don noticed. 'I had a battle with her in the beginning, but I can control her now.'

'I'm sure you can. Look, I've brought you something. I was going to give it to your mother to give to you later, but now you're here . . .' Patrick took a small package out of his pocket and gave it to Judy. She opened it carefully.

'It's perfume,' she said in a flat voice. Don noticed it was a very expensive one.

'For a young woman who's becoming as beautiful as her mother.' Patrick smiled.

'Thanks,' Judy said quietly and put the perfume in her pocket.

Don felt angry. Who did this Forsha think he was, coming out to the airfield like this and giving his daughter presents in front of him?

Forsha turned to Sylvia. 'Well, are you ready?' he asked. 'I thought we'd have dinner in Brisbane and then go down to the Gold Coast after that, if that's OK.'

'Gold Coast?' Don asked.

'Patrick has invited me to his new hotel on the Gold Coast for a few days,' Sylvia said, looking away.

'Yes,' said Forsha, 'and I have a meeting before dinner, so we must be off. It was nice to meet you again, Don.' He turned and walked back towards the helicopter.

Sylvia turned to look at Don.

'I'm sorry,' she said, and turned to Judy. 'Have a good time darling. I'll call you at Paul's tonight.'

She looked at Don and started to say something, but stopped herself. She kissed her daughter on the cheek and followed Patrick, leaving Don and Judy alone together.

Judy spoke first, 'I don't like perfume. He's always buying me presents I don't want.'

'Keep it,' said Don. 'You might use it one day.' He

turned to look at his daughter. 'Has . . . has that man – Mr Forsha – been seeing your mum a lot?'

Judy looked unhappy. 'For about six months. She met him on a trip to the city, I think. Sometimes he flies out to the farm. I think he wants to marry her.'

Don looked at his daughter. She had grown up so much while he was away. She was changing fast, and he felt he didn't know her any more. He didn't know what sort of things she liked now, or how she felt.

'Do you want him to marry your mother?' he asked.

Judy shook her head and looked at her father. 'I don't like him very much. And . . . ' She stopped.

'And what?'

'He frightens me.'

Chapter 3 *The Sugar Glider*

Paul Copeman appeared at the office door and looked out. 'OK, I'm finished,' he said. 'I thought we could have a quick look at the DC4, Don. Have you told Judy about our plans?' he asked.

'No, not yet.' Don replied. Judy looked at him questioningly. 'Judy, we'll have to wait a couple of days before we do any trips in my new plane,' her father said. 'Paul and I have a small job to do.'

'Oh, Dad,' Judy said sadly.

'Don't worry, Judy,' said Paul. 'You can stay with Beulah at the house, and we'll be back before you know it.'

'OK,' Judy nodded, but she still looked unhappy.

Paul put his arm around her and pointed across the airfield at the DC4. 'We're flying that lovely old plane to Melbourne. It's called the *Sugar Glider*. Come on, let's all go and have a look.'

Together they walked across the airfield towards the plane. Its shape threw a long shadow in the afternoon sun. A ladder stood against it. A painted line went from the nose of the plane back along the roof. There were two great propeller engines on each wing. Oil was falling slowly in drops from one of the engines.

'Is that normal?' Judy asked, pointing at a large tray under the wing filling with oil.

Paul laughed. 'It's like an old car. It uses a lot of oil, but it's OK. This is a plane with history. It's had a lot of adventures.'

'Really?' said Judy. 'What like?'

'Well,' Paul said, 'it was made in America, and first used for carrying American soldiers in the Second World War. Then a private company bought it, and used it to carry coffee from South America. Later it went to an Asian country. It used to be a president's private plane.'

'How do you know all this?' Judy asked.

'Every plane has a record of its history, of every flight. It's called the log book,' Don told her.

'Can we look inside?' Judy said.

'Of course, let's go,' said Paul.

Don was pleased that Judy was showing an interest in the plane. He pulled open the heavy door to the cockpit, where the pilots sat. The controls were much simpler than in modern planes. There was plenty of room in the cockpit, with two seats for the pilots, and two more seats behind. Don, Paul and Judy went back through a door into the plane and found a heavy wooden table and black leather chairs fixed to the floor.

'This was the president's meeting room, I suppose,' said Don. 'Let's see what else we can find.'

They went through another door to the back of the plane, which was mostly empty space. There were cupboards on either side. Judy opened one, and was surprised to see some cans inside. They looked quite old. They were cans of soup, beans and other vegetables.

'What are these for?' she said.

'Someone must have left them. Emergency food supplies maybe,' said Don, looking over her shoulder.

Judy noticed a set of holes along the floor. 'What are those?' she asked.

'There were seats here before,' said Paul. 'I told you the plane used to carry people as well as things.

'And why is it called the *Sugar Glider*?' Judy asked. 'That's the name of an Australian animal.'

She pictured the strange animal with its bright eyes, thick tail, and the black line down its body. So that was why they had painted the line on the plane. She had seen a sugar glider once, on holiday in the north Queensland rainforest. She remembered the yip-yip-yip noise it had made.

'Well, it wasn't called that at first,' said Paul. 'I told you it was a president's private plane. An Australian pilot, John Henderson, used to work for him. But there was a war in the president's country. The government was losing the war, and Henderson flew the president to safety in Australia. So he gave the plane to Henderson as a thank-you present. Henderson started his own company, carrying things all over Australia, but now the plane's getting too old, so he's just sold it to the Melbourne Air Museum. That's where we're taking it, for its last trip.'

'Wow, it's been everywhere. I wish I could fly in it!' said Judy.

Don had a sudden thought. Maybe Judy could come with them on the trip to Melbourne. He decided to speak to Paul about it later.

Chapter 4 *An argument*

Paul and Beulah Copeman's house was a blue and white 'Queenslander', a wooden house painted white with green edges. A jacaranda tree was dropping purple flowers onto the garden. Paul parked in front of the house and they went up the front steps. Paul's wife Beulah came to meet them.

She took Judy's arm. 'My goodness,' she said, 'how you've grown! And Don! You haven't changed at all!'

'How have you been, Beulah?' Don said.

'Fine, Don. I'm so glad you're back. We've missed you. Come inside' she said.

They all went in and Don looked around the house. He knew it so well: the pictures of aeroplanes on the walls; the large shelves with glass doors. Here too, small metal or plastic planes of all kinds could be seen behind the glass. Everything was very neat and tidy.

No children, thought Don. He thought it was a pity. Children always liked Paul and Beulah, and they had always been very special people for Judy.

'Why don't you men sit out in the shade?' Beulah suggested. 'And Judy, you can have a shower if you like. You must be hot after that long drive.'

'Thanks, I will.' Judy followed Beulah out of the room.

'Come outside, Don. I expect you'd like a beer,' Paul said. He took two bottles from the fridge and led Don to the back of the house. They sat down on wooden chairs on the deck, a raised covered area outside. Below the deck was a small, neat garden. Two beautifully coloured birds came and sat on the wall.

'So, Don, will you enjoy being back, do you think?'

'I think so, Paul. I had a good job in the islands; it's a peaceful kind of life. But when you called, I realised how much I missed home.'

'And your family.' added Paul.

'Of course. I left in such a hurry, didn't I?' Don said. 'After the divorce I just wanted to get away. Now I feel I have to get to know Judy all over again. At the moment, I'm finding it a bit difficult to know what to say to her.'

'Well, Don, it's early days,' Paul said. 'I can see she's glad you're back. She needs a father. It was such a pity about you and Sylvia. Brisbane's loveliest couple, I always thought.' He smiled sadly.

'When you asked me to come back and start the flying school . . . ' Don began.

'Yes?'

'I don't know; I hoped there might be another chance to work things out with Sylvia.'

'I hope so too,' said Paul. 'It's no secret that I've always wanted to help both of you. I think you both need another chance.'

Don frowned. 'But it looks like I might be too late.'

'What makes you say that?' Paul asked.

'That helicopter that came in to the airfield this afternoon,' Don explained to his friend, 'belonged to Sylvia's new boyfriend. He's taken her off to the Gold Coast for the weekend. Judy seems to think it's quite serious.'

'What's his name?'

'Forsha. Patrick Forsha. Have you heard of him?' Don asked.

'Yes, I have. He's a businessman. A real smooth type. He likes to show off his money,' Paul answered.

'Exactly. He gave Judy an expensive present in front of me and he made a point of telling me that he's bought her a horse.'

Paul frowned. 'Yes. That sounds just like him. Well, I thought Sylvia looked pleased to see you. Maybe you two can spend some time together after this job. Talk things over.'

'Mm. Let's hope so,' said Don.

* * *

That same evening, not far away in Brisbane's city centre, Sylvia was sitting alone in an expensive Italian restaurant called Mario's. Patrick had gone to answer a telephone call, while Sylvia was drinking a glass of wine and thinking.

Mario's had been Patrick's idea. He didn't know that when she was married to Don it had been their favourite restaurant. Memories came back of the times she and Don had laughed together there over romantic dinners. She looked at the beautiful pictures of Italy on the walls. She and Don had gone to Italy for their honeymoon. They had had a good life together. What had gone wrong? At the airfield, old feelings had started to come back, but then Patrick had arrived. She hadn't wanted Don and Patrick to meet but she hadn't known the demonstrations would make her and Judy so late.

She looked at her watch. It was eight o'clock – time to call Judy. She rang Paul and Beulah's number on her mobile. Just at that moment Don was passing the Copemans' phone on his way into the kitchen for another beer.

'Get that, will you, Don,' shouted Paul from the deck.

'Oh, Don,' Sylvia said, surprised. 'It's you. This is Sylvia. I was just calling Judy . . . '

'Hello, Sylvia,' Don said, and his heart jumped. 'Are you calling from the Gold Coast?'

'No, we're still in Brisbane,' she replied. 'Patrick's making a business call.' She paused. 'Don, I'm sorry about today.'

'Sorry for what? It's none of my business,' Don replied, a little too angrily.

There was a moment's silence and then Sylvia said quietly, 'Don, you left me, remember? I've been lonely.'

'Yes, I know. So have I,' he replied. There was a long silence this time. 'I'll get Judy,' he said, finally.

Judy came to the phone. 'Mum?' she said.

'Hi, darling. Are you all right?'

'I'm fine, Mum.'

'Well, I'm going down to the coast tonight, but I'll be back soon.'

'You can stay a bit longer at the coast if you want, Mum. I'm staying here with Beulah. Dad and Paul are going to Melbourne.'

'What do you mean?' her mother asked.

'They've got some kind of flying job. They're taking an old plane to a museum, or something.'

Sylvia couldn't believe it. She had driven all the way to Brisbane so Judy could see her father and now he was going off flying. 'Darling, I'll call you tomorrow. Put your father back on the phone, please.'

'Sylvia?' Don's voice came back on the line.

'This sounds just like you, Don Radcliffe. You haven't seen Judy for a year, and then you take the first chance to go off flying – without her,' Sylvia said angrily.

'It's only two days. It's an important job.'

'Oh yes, of course it is. Flying is always more important than family. You haven't changed, Don. I hoped . . . I hoped things would be different.'

'I'm sorry,' said Don, 'but it's really not very long.'

'That's what you always said, but you were never at home.'

'Sylvia, please . . .'

'Goodbye, Don. Tell Judy I'll call tomorrow evening.' She hung up, and put the phone back in her handbag. Patrick was coming back to the table. She didn't want him to see that she was upset but she needn't have worried. He looked upset himself. He sat down, a little out of breath.

'Anything wrong?' she asked.

He shook his head. 'I just had a few business problems to solve. Nothing important,' he said. 'Come on now. Let's relax.'

Sylvia looked at him. 'Patrick, Don's going to Melbourne tomorrow and leaving Judy here in Brisbane. I think I should stay here with her.'

Patrick looked at her. 'Well, I must say that sounds typical of him,' he said with a cold smile. 'It's just like when he left you.'

'I've told you before, it wasn't quite like that,' Sylvia interrupted. 'It was my fault too. I wasn't very patient.'

'And now he's back,' Patrick said quietly, 'expecting you to be patient again. Sylvia, can we just forget about Don? I don't want to talk about him; I want to talk about you and me. You know how I feel about you.' He took her hand in his. 'I want to marry you, Sylvia.'

'Patrick, you're very kind,' Sylvia said, looking at the table, 'but . . . I don't know. I feel very confused at the moment. You must give me time.'

Patrick held her hand more tightly. 'I'm sorry. I don't want to push you,' he said softly. 'It's just that I care so much about you – and Judy of course.'

'Thank you,' Sylvia said. 'You've been good to us, I know.'

'Look, please come to my new hotel on the Gold Coast. I know we could have a special time together.'

Sylvia looked up at him, tears in her eyes. 'I don't know.'

'Please,' he said, looking straight into her eyes.

'All right,' said Sylvia. 'I'll come with you.'

He smiled and looked at his watch. 'I'll get the car,' he said.

* * *

After Don put the phone down, he thought about what Sylvia had said. She was right, he knew. He had always put flying first. That was why they had got divorced. Now he was doing the same thing to his daughter. It was a bad start to his return home. He went back outside.

Paul was alone on the deck. 'The girls are making coffee,' he said. Then he saw the expression on his friend's face. 'Problems, Don?' he asked.

Don nodded. 'Paul, I've been thinking,' he said. 'Why don't we take Judy with us to Melbourne?'

Paul looked worried. 'I don't know, Don. It'll be a long uncomfortable trip. She'd be better here with Beulah.'

'She won't be a problem. I want her to come, Paul. In fact, if she doesn't come, I'm going to say no to your offer. Judy and I have been apart too long already.'

Paul thought hard. His friend seemed to have made up his mind. Don wouldn't do the job if Judy didn't come, and if he didn't do the job, they wouldn't get the money for the flying school.

'OK, Don,' Paul said at last. 'If Judy wants to come, of course she can.'

'Come where?' Judy had come out with a tray. She put it down on the table. Don put his hand on her shoulder. 'Judy, do you want to come with us to Melbourne? In the *Sugar Glider*?'

Judy's eyes lit up. 'Yes, please!'

'OK. You'll need to get your things ready tonight,' Don said. 'OK, Paul?'

Paul smiled. 'There's a backpack in the cupboard in your room. You can put a few overnight clothes for the trip in that.'

'I'm going to pack now!' said Judy, excited. Paul watched her run back inside. He hoped there wouldn't be any problems.

Chapter 5 *Take off*

Judy had a dream. She was sitting in the cockpit of the *Sugar Glider,* next to her father. The plane was moving slowly down the runway. She turned to ask her father something, but now Patrick was in the pilot's seat, not her father. Patrick was grinning, but his eyes were black and empty. She started screaming. 'Let me out! I want to get out!' She got up and went to the cockpit door. Her father was lying by the door, and his eyes were closed. Judy pushed the door, but it wouldn't open. Patrick turned round and shouted, 'It's too late!' She pushed and pushed until the door finally opened. The plane was going too fast to jump, but she looked out. Two trucks were racing after the plane. The men were in uniform, and they had guns.

'You see, my dear, we have to get away,' shouted Patrick, laughing wildly.

The first truck was nearly level with them. One of the men stood up and threw something at the plane.

'It's a bomb!' Judy thought. The object went past her, and landed inside the plane. The plane's nose started to lift. Judy held onto the door. She couldn't move.

She woke up, sweating. The time on the clock next to her bed was seven o'clock. Time to get up. She went to the bathroom and put cold water on her face.

'I'm just excited about the journey,' she thought. Her imagination had mixed up the events of the last twenty-four hours: Paul's stories about the *Sugar Glider*, seeing her father again, her feelings about her father, and about Patrick. She got dressed, picked up the backpack and hurried out to the deck for breakfast.

Paul and Don were already on the deck, eating toast and drinking coffee. The morning was fresh and bright, and birds were singing in the trees. Judy felt much calmer.

'Ready for the adventure, Judy?' Don touched her hand and held it for a moment. He was always happy when he was going to fly, and to share the trip in such an interesting plane with his daughter would make this a day to remember.

At the airfield, the *Sugar Glider* stood alone, silver in the morning sun.

'We'd better do the flight plan,' Don said.

'I've already done it,' Paul told him.

Don looked at him. 'I'll take it to the office, if you like,' he said.

'It's OK, Don, you can start checking the controls. I'll take in the plan and then I'll fly first, if that's OK.' Paul didn't give Don time to reply, but quickly turned and walked towards the office. Don watched him go, puzzled. Paul seemed nervous and in a hurry. It wasn't like him.

Don and Judy walked over to the plane and climbed in. The airfield was quiet. A few minutes later Paul joined them in the cockpit.

'Can I see a copy of the flight plan? I want to check where we're going,' said Don. Paul took a sheet of paper from his case and handed it to his friend.

'Warrangi's a few hours flying time to the northwest,' Paul answered. 'Quite far inland.'

'So we're flying over some very empty country,' said Don as he checked the radio and called up the control tower.

'That's true,' Paul replied.

Fifteen minutes later, and with all the checks completed, the big propellers slowly began to move. As they turned faster, the engines got louder. Paul took the *Sugar Glider* down to the end of the runway. A voice on the radio announced that they could take off. Although she had her seat belt on, Judy held tightly onto her seat. She had a jacket on her knees. She would need it when they were high in the air. The *Sugar Glider* was not a modern plane with heating; it could get cold up there.

They were off the ground. Everett's Field filled the window, then they saw streets and houses getting smaller and smaller. Within minutes the city disappeared, and all they could see was the green landscape. The hills near Brisbane were covered with trees.

The plane reached its flying height of just over six thousand meters and levelled out. Don turned round. 'OK, Judy?' he said. His daughter smiled back.

'Can I leave my seat now?'

'OK. We've got good weather, but come back and sit down if it gets rough,' Don told her.

Judy got up and went through the door, past the wooden table and leather chairs, towards the back of the plane. She looked out of the window for a few minutes.

Australia is so big and empty, she thought. It's so far between the towns and cities. She remembered at school what she had studied about the first explorers who had come from Europe. Many of them had had no idea of the size of the country; they had got lost, and died in the huge empty spaces that Australians called the outback.

Curious, she looked in the cupboards. There were the cans of food she had seen the day before. As she opened another cupboard, she heard a noise behind her. Her father had come to the back.

'Found anything interesting?' he asked her.

'Look, Dad. There's lots of stuff in here,' she said. 'What's it for?'

Don came over and looked inside. He saw some rope, knives, a saw, and a few other tools. All of them looked old.

Don shook his head. 'The plane was used to carry things, so rope would be useful. The other stuff I don't know. Maybe workmen left it behind.'

'The cupboards are very smelly too.' Judy made a face.

'You could use the perfume that Mr Forsha gave you. Do you still have it?'

She felt in her pocket. 'Yes.'

Don was thoughtful. 'Judy, yesterday you said Mr Forsha scared you.'

'I don't want to talk about him.' Judy looked at the floor.

'OK, I'm sorry.'

Judy looked into his eyes. 'Dad, why did you go away? Mum's been so lonely.'

Don shook his head. 'She told me. I'm very sorry that I hurt you both.'

He changed the subject. 'Look, you're getting cold. Go back to the cockpit; it's warmer there. Get Paul to show you the controls. I want to see what else is back here.' He didn't want to talk about the past. He knew he'd made mistakes, but at least Judy was here with him now.

Back in the cockpit, Paul invited her to sit in the co-pilot's seat.

'The controls aren't really that difficult,' Paul told her. 'You could fly most planes with one hand.'

'Are helicopters easy too?' She was thinking of Patrick's visit to the airfield.

'They're different. I've never flown one, but I know you always need both hands to land and take off. So it's best not to disturb a helicopter pilot at those times!'

'I'd like to learn to fly,' Judy said.

'Well, if your dad and I get this flying school started . . .' Paul smiled at her.

Don came back to the cockpit, so Judy went behind and sat in one of the leather chairs. She had brought some magazines with her, so she settled down to read.

Two hours later they were preparing to come down. 'It's time to speak to the mine,' Paul said. Don touched a switch, and a noise came from the radio. Then he spoke.

'This is the *Sugar Glider* calling Warrangi. Over.'

A voice answered: 'This is Warrangi Airfield, *Sugar Glider*. Where are you?'

'About fifty kilometers southeast. We're coming down in a few minutes.'

'*Sugar Glider,* don't land at the airfield. Come in about two kilometers to the west. It's flat there, no rocks or trees. We'll get a service truck out to you. You'll need more fuel.'

'Why can't we land at your airfield?' Don asked.

'We've got big problems today. You'll see when you get close. It's not a good day for you to come, so I'd be pleased if you didn't waste my time asking questions.'

Don looked out of the window. Soon he could see some low buildings in the distance, the fence round the mine area, and a road leading to it. There was a line of cars and trucks all along the road. The plane circled the area, getting lower and lower. Now Don could see a lot of people at the mine entrance. 'What are they all doing here?' Don wondered.

'They must be demonstrators like the ones we saw yesterday,' Judy said. 'The Warrangi Mine's on Murri land. The Murri were moved off there years ago. The government promised they would close the mine down and give it back to them.'

'So why haven't they closed it yet?' her father asked.

Paul answered this question. 'I was reading about it in the paper yesterday. The mine owners still get some iron and other metals from the mine, but now they think there might be other minerals in the area. So the government is trying to keep it open a bit longer. At least that's what people are saying.'

'Yeah. The Murri people are very angry about it,' Judy added. 'They think the government has broken its promise. A lot of people have been coming from all over Australia.'

'And does our job today have anything to do with this?' Don asked.

'I'm not sure, Don,' Paul answered, and he looked away out of the window.

Chapter 6 *Warrangi Mine*

The *Sugar Glider* came to a stop on a flat, dry plain. It was just after eleven in the morning. They had been flying for a little over two hours. As the engines died away, they could hear singing in the distance. It was too far away to hear the words, but Don recognised the song. The people outside the mine were singing a popular song by Midnight Oil, an Australian rock band.

In a few minutes an open truck arrived with a ladder in the back. Two men got out and put the ladder against the plane. Paul came down first. One of the men who was tall and wearing black shorts, came forward. He wasn't smiling.

'Ned Manderville, mine manager. You've come on a lively day, no mistake!'

'Too right. I'm Paul Copeman.' The two men shook hands and Paul gave the manager the envelope. 'How soon can we get the stuff and move on?' Paul asked him.

'There'll be a bit of a delay. The newspaper and TV people are here. I've got to talk to them in a minute. Everyone will have their say, and after that we hope the police can get these damned demonstrators to go away quietly. Oh, you've got a passenger.' He frowned. Judy was coming down the ladder behind Don, magazine in hand.

'I'm Don Radcliffe. This is my daughter Judy,' said Don.

'I didn't know anyone else was coming. It's not very convenient, with all this going on.' Manderville waved towards the mine.

'You don't have to worry. Bring the equipment and we'll be out of here,' Paul said.

'I'll send the fuel truck and your equipment out here as soon as I can,' Manderville said. 'We'll have to go back to the office and sort the papers out. You'd all better come inside the gates for safety. I really didn't need this today.'

They got in the back of the truck. The police cleared the way for them to go through the gates and they were soon at the office.

'I'll have to ask your daughter to wait outside the office,' Manderville said.

'Do you mind, Judy?' Paul said.

'No, that's OK. I'll read my magazine,' Judy replied.

'Maybe you'd better wait outside too, Don, just in case there's any trouble. I'll be as quick as I can,' Paul said.

'OK,' Don answered. Paul followed Manderville into the office.

Judy found a rock in the shade and sat down to read her magazine. It was a hot afternoon. One of the demonstrators began to make a speech, and a lot of people were shouting. Judy looked up and saw the TV cameras pointing at the crowd, then at the mine. She got up and walked along the fence.

'What are you doing behind the fence, lady?' a voice called out. 'You should be on this side!' Judy looked around. Lady? The voice belonged to a good-looking, brown-skinned Murri boy of about eighteen. His smile was friendly.

'I'm just visiting,' she said. 'We've got nothing to do with the mine, but I understand why you're demonstrating.'

'Ah, what do you know about it?' said the youth.

'I live on a farm,' she said. 'I understand how important land is to you. I hope you get what you want.' Then she turned and walked back towards her father, who was standing alone in front of the office. The boy's eyes followed her.

The shouting from the demonstrators increased as the manager came outside with a group of men and walked to the gate. Cameras and reporters surrounded Manderville, and Judy couldn't hear his words above the noise. Paul came out soon after, carrying a brown envelope. He walked over to Don and Judy. He was red-faced in the heat.

'Are those the papers for the equipment? Can I see them?' Don asked.

Paul handed over the envelope. 'There's not much to see,' he said. Don opened the envelope and took out some sheets of paper. He frowned as he looked at them. There was no description, nothing to tell them what they were supposed to be carrying, just some numbers.

'What is this? We could be carrying anything. What are these numbers?' Don asked, but Paul didn't answer. He was looking towards the gate.

Manderville had finished speaking. The TV people were packing up, and the police were starting to move people away. Don saw three large trucks moving towards the gate. The first one, driven by a tall thin man in mechanic's clothes, was a fuel truck for the *Sugar Glider*, Don supposed. In another he could see some lifting equipment. The third truck carried several wooden boxes and six round metal containers – long round black cases, with nothing written on them, Don noticed. As the fuel truck passed them, the driver looked at Don for a moment, then looked away quickly. Don turned back to Paul.

'Paul, I asked you something. What are we carrying, exactly?'

'I told you yesterday. It's equipment and chemicals,' Paul said.

Don looked at his friend, who was sweating a lot. 'Are you sure you've told me everything, Paul?' Don asked.

'Don, they're paying us a lot of money to do this job and not ask questions. We'll be out of here soon, and it'll all be over. Just think about the flying school.'

'Paul, do you know something I don't? Is this job safe? I brought Judy along, remember?' Don asked, anxiously.

Paul smiled weakly. 'Of course it's safe.'

Another man came out of the mine office and spoke to them. 'Sorry about the wait. You must be thirsty. Come and have a drink. They're putting your stuff on the plane now.'

As they walked back to the truck, Don looked again at his friend.

'You don't look too good, Paul. Are you OK?' he asked.

'I'm fine. It's just the heat,' Paul replied.

But despite Paul's reply, Don began to feel more and more uncomfortable. He just wanted to finish the job and get back to Brisbane.

Chapter 7 *Forced landing*

It was just after midday. Most of the demonstrators had gone, and the *Sugar Glider* was ready for take-off. Manderville came out of the office with another man.

'OK, everything's on board. It's time for you to get going,' Manderville told them. 'Ted here will take you back to your plane.' He turned his back and walked away without another word.

They drove back to the plane in the same open truck. It was quiet now. They checked the boxes and containers in the back to make sure they were tightly tied down. As he took the plane's controls, Don wondered what kind of chemicals were inside. It was his turn to fly. Paul called the mine on the *Sugar Glider*'s radio. A voice answered: 'There's nothing around for miles now. Take off when you want.'

In a few minutes they were up again, in the clear sky.

'I'll just check the flight plan,' said Don. 'We lost some time at the mine. Maybe we can make it up.' Paul handed him a sheet of paper without saying a word. Paul had been acting very strangely since they had arrived at the mine, Don thought.

'Your plan takes us a long way west, Paul,' Don said.

'I wanted to avoid the mountains. There are a lot of storms at the moment,' Paul answered.

'The weather looks fine. We'll make up time if we fly over the mountains.'

'Breaking the rules, Don?' Paul said quietly.

'You taught me to break rules, Paul.'

'I suppose I did,' Paul said.

Don set a new course southeast. 'Are you OK, Judy?' he asked. His daughter had been very quiet.

'I'm fine, Dad. I was just thinking about the people outside the mine. I talked to a boy there.'

'Oh yes?' Don turned round to look at her.

'He was a Murri. I was just thinking about his people. I hope they get Warrangi back. It's not fair.'

'You're right, but sometimes life isn't very fair,' Don said. He realised Judy had grown up so much in a year. Now she had opinions; she cared about important things. He had never thought much about land rights. He had always been more interested in the air than the ground.

An hour and a half later the landscape changed to a darker green as they flew over the mountains of the Great Dividing Range. Suddenly the engines made a loud coughing noise. The plane shook.

'Strange, the outside fuel tanks can't be empty yet. But I'll switch tanks anyway,' said Don. He leaned forward and moved a switch. 'We should have a smooth flight now until Melbourne,' he added.

'How long will it take?' asked Judy.

'Still about three and a half hours,' Don told her. 'We can't go as fast as a jet . . . ' He stopped. There was a loud noise from outside the plane. The engines coughed again, the *Sugar Glider* shook violently, then dropped suddenly. Judy felt sick to her stomach.

Don looked at the controls. 'We're losing height fast,' he said.

'What's going on? You've just switched tanks!' Paul said.

'I know, but there's something wrong. We're dropping. I'm trying to keep the nose up,' Don said.

Judy's face was very pale. 'Are we going to crash?' she asked in a weak voice.

'Not if we can help it,' Don said. He thought fast. 'I'll have to look for somewhere to land. Judy, go behind and put a belt on. You'll be safer in that part of the plane. The landing might be rough. Don't worry. We'll be OK.' Don had to concentrate hard, and he did not want Judy to panic.

Judy did as she was told. 'I'll radio our position,' Don said when Judy had gone. He pushed a button. But he could hear no sound at all.

'I can't get through. Something's wrong with the radio. What's going on?' Don looked at Paul. His friend's chest was rising and falling fast, and his face was white. They were still dropping fast.

'The propellers, Don,' Paul said in a whisper. He pointed at a button on the controls.

It had been a long time since Don had flown such an old propeller plane, but now he remembered the special button which would help them stay level if the engines stopped. He pressed it, and the sides of the propellers changed position. This made the wind turn them, so that the plane could glide safely downwards. The *Sugar Glider* was living up to its name. Don looked at the ground coming closer, and searched desperately for somewhere to land. He saw smoke rising somewhere in the distance. 'It's probably a farm, but I don't think I can get that far,' he thought.

Because he had changed course, they were over hills covered with thick bush. He turned away to the left and saw a wider valley. There were still plenty of trees, but there might be enough flat land to get down safely. He could hear the wind screaming outside. The ground was coming up to meet them. 'Hold tight everybody!' Don shouted.

With a tremendous bang they were down on the valley floor. Don desperately tried to avoid trees and stones, but a large rock appeared in front of them. There was a loud noise as one of the landing wheels broke. The plane went down on one side and turned suddenly to the left. Then the other wheel broke. The plane was now moving along on its body, still fast and out of control. They were approaching a thick group of trees. Some branches caught one wing. The shock turned the plane round violently, bringing trees and branches crashing down on top of them. Everything went dark as the plane finally came to rest.

There was a heavy silence. Don felt his arms and legs. It seemed nothing was broken. He heard the calls of birds, then a weak sound next to him.

'Paul?'

'Don, I'm sorry,' Paul said. His voice was very weak.

'Don't be sorry. We're down, Paul. We're OK.'

'No, we're not OK,' Paul said.

'What do you mean? What's going on?' Don asked.

'I took the job for the money, for our flying school . . . because of you, Don,' Paul said. 'I knew you weren't happy alone. I wanted you to come home, get back with your family. I didn't think anything could go wrong.'

Don looked at his friend. He felt Paul's chest. His heartbeat was very weak.

'At the mine,' Paul continued, 'I found out . . . those containers . . . We're carrying uranium, Don.'

Don was silent. Uranium, he thought. So that's why the mine hasn't closed yet. They found uranium. It's worth a lot of money to someone, for power stations to make electricity, or . . . he realised with a shock, bombs.

'But why would the government get us to carry . . .' he began.

'I don't think it was a government job at all,' Paul said in a small voice. 'I think we've been tricked.'

'What do you mean? Who was it, if it wasn't the government?' Don asked.'

'I don't know, but those men at Warrangi, they did something to the plane . . . forced us down . . . This crash wasn't an accident, Don. I'm sure of it. They never intended us to get to Melbourne.' Paul's face was turning blue. 'I've been so stupid. I should have known: the way they didn't want Warrangi on the flight plan, how they knew so much about us. Be careful Don . . .'

'Careful? Who do you mean, "they"?' Don said, but Paul's mouth opened and his head fell forward.

Chapter 8 *Lost in the outback*

It was almost dark in the cockpit. Don gently pushed Paul's head back and felt his chest again. This time there was no heartbeat.

Don called to Judy in the back. 'Are you OK, Judy?'

'I think so,' she answered. The door opened. Judy came into the cockpit, carefully feeling her way.

'What about you, Dad?'

'Judy, I'm fine, but Paul . . .'

'What's happened? Is he hurt?' she asked.

'Judy, I'm afraid Paul's dead.'

Judy began to cry. Don took off his seat belt and got up slowly. He found Judy and held her tightly, feeling her tears fall onto his shirt.

'I think he had a heart attack,' Don said, remembering Paul's breathing problems and the strange way he had been acting.

'What are we going to do?' Judy cried.

'First of all, we've got to get out of here,' Don said. He tried to open the cockpit door, but it would not move.

'There must be trees blocking it on the outside,' Don said. 'We'll have to get out through the back. Come on.'

They made their way to the back of the plane. There was more light there from the windows. Some of the wooden boxes had come loose, but the metal containers were still in place. Don checked them all. None of them seemed to be broken.

They moved towards the door at the back of the plane. Don found a handle and turned it, but the door opened only a little way. There were branches against it. But more light poured in, enough for them to see what they were doing.

'OK Judy, can you squeeze through?' Don asked. He pushed hard against the door, and managed to move it enough for Judy to climb out. With a big effort he got through after her. Branches scratched their faces and hands.

'Right, now get away from the plane,' Don said to his daughter. 'I just want to check something.'

'Please hurry,' Judy said. She was shaking despite the warm late afternoon weather. With difficulty Don made his way round to the fuel tanks and opened the cover. There was a strong smell of fuel. If there was fuel inside, why had the engines stopped? He smelled again, carefully. It was a familiar smell, but he realized it wasn't the right fuel for the plane. It was jet fuel. Mechanics wouldn't make a mistake like that. With this discovery, Don now knew that Paul had been right. It had been done on purpose. Mixing the fuels had caused the engines to stop. Somebody at the mine had wanted to bring the plane down in the outback and didn't care what happened to Paul, Judy and himself. Whoever it was wanted the uranium, and if they had seen the *Sugar Glider*'s flight plan, they would know where to look for the plane later. 'But,' Don thought, 'I changed course. So they won't be able to find the plane immediately.'

And, without a radio, he quickly realised, rescuers wouldn't be able to find him and Judy either. The flight plan they had would be completely wrong!

They needed to get going before it got dark, but before

Don left the plane there was something else he had to find out. He climbed up the broken trees and onto the roof. The radio aerial was not there. It had broken off. He touched the place where it had been and felt his hand burning. Of course! Someone at the mine had put a chemical on the aerial: some kind of acid to weaken it. So, when they were flying the wind had easily broken it off. These people really knew what they were doing, Don thought.

He got down from the roof and went after Judy. He found her sitting by a rock, staring at the ground. 'We didn't crash by accident,' he told her.

'Oh?' she said in a dull voice. Her eyes were lifeless, and she was still shaking. 'She's in shock,' Don thought. He put his arms around her for a few moments.

He looked around. They were at the bottom of a wide valley. About fifty meters away he could see the shine of water. The *Sugar Glider* had crashed into a thick forest. Trees, rocks and the side of the valley hid most of the plane. It could hardly be seen from where they were now. From the air it would be difficult to see it at all.

'Judy, listen carefully,' Don said. 'They put uranium on the plane at Warrangi. Do you know what that is?'

Judy's eyes opened wide. 'Of course I do. They make bombs with it.'

'We didn't know that was what they wanted us to carry. Paul found out at the mine, but he didn't tell me. I wouldn't have left the mine if I'd known.'

Judy nodded, and Don went on, 'it doesn't matter now. The important thing is that somebody at the mine did something to the plane. They wanted to force us down so they could pick up the uranium in secret. They probably think they can find us easily.'

'But you changed course. I heard you talking to Paul. They won't find us. Nobody will find us.' She was shaking again.

'Rescuers will come looking eventually. When we don't arrive in Melbourne on time, they'll report us as missing,' Don said. He hoped that he sounded more confident than he felt.

Judy looked back towards the plane. She saw the trees and said, 'The plane's covered. No one could see us from the air! We'll have to make a fire.'

'Wait,' Don warned her. 'We don't know who'll come first, rescuers or the people who want the uranium, and they might think we know too much. We have to be careful.'

'So we're lost, but we can't make a signal. We might die here,' said Judy. A bird made a loud noise nearby, making her jump. 'Why did you bring me here?' she shouted.

Don hung his head. Judy was right to feel angry. He had left home when she needed a father and hadn't seen her for a year. Now he was back, and the first thing he had done was to lead her into danger.

'Judy, I'm so sorry,' he said. But his daughter had stopped listening. She started screaming into the emptiness.

Chapter 9 *Rescuers?*

Don did nothing. Being angry was good, he thought. It would help Judy to recover from the shock of everything that had happened. At last she came to him and cried in his arms.

'Come down to the creek,' he told her. They walked down to the water's edge. He knelt down to put water on his face and drink from the stream. Judy got on her knees and did the same. As she drank, Judy realised they were both lucky to be alive. She looked around. The valley was thick with trees on both sides. They heard the noises of strange birds. It was a beautiful afternoon.

'Are you OK now?' Don asked, and his daughter nodded. 'I'm going to get some things from the plane. If it hasn't blown up by now, I think it's safe.'

'Don't leave me here, Dad. I'll help,' Judy said.

She followed him back to the *Sugar Glider*. They took out the cans of food, the rope and any tools they could carry, and put them in their backpacks. Judy found two boxes of matches and an old pair of binoculars in one of the cupboards. Before they left the *Sugar Glider* for the last time, Don found a sheet of heavy plastic. He took it to the cockpit and gently covered Paul's body.

'Goodbye, old friend. I don't blame you for this,' he whispered. Paul had been more than a friend; he had been Don's teacher, too.

'Why did he take such a risk with this job?' Don asked

himself, but he knew the answer. 'For the flying school. To help me find a way to be with Judy and Sylvia again.'

'I've made too many decisions in my life out of selfishness,' Don thought. He promised himself that if they got away, he would always be there for Judy from now on.

When they were a safe distance from the plane, Don suggested leaving their backpacks and climbing to the top of the valley.

'We need to get a better idea of the area before it gets dark,' he said. 'Bring those binoculars.'

It was hard going at first. The bushes were thick, and large black flies bothered them. It took twenty minutes to reach the top. To the west they could see it was flatter, with fewer trees. To the east the mountains stretched away, covered in thick bush.

'Where do you think we are, Dad?' Judy asked, breathing hard.

'Somewhere in central eastern New South Wales. That's where we should be, after I changed course.'

The noise of an engine interrupted the peace of the late afternoon. They turned towards the sound. A helicopter appeared over the other side of the valley.

'Quick, get down,' Don said. They ran under the cover of the trees. The helicopter went up and down the valley several times.

'Are you sure they haven't come to rescue us?' Judy asked.

'I don't like it,' said Don. 'It's too soon for rescuers to be looking for us. We're not even supposed to be in Melbourne yet.'

Judy looked down the hillside. The helicopter was flying

away from them towards some moving shapes on the floor of the valley. She held the binoculars to her eyes.

'Look, Dad. There are kangaroos down there; they're coming out to drink at the creek. The helicopter's going towards them. They're moving away.'

'Give me the binoculars,' said Don. He watched the helicopter come nearer. He could see two men inside. One of the men was carrying a gun. His figure was familiar. Don thought he had seen the man at Warrangi.

'What can you see?' Judy asked.

Suddenly shots echoed around the valley. The kangaroos jumped off in all directions. Then the helicopter rose quickly and flew away to the west. Don wondered what kind of people found it amusing to frighten such gentle animals.

'Rescuers don't shoot at kangaroos,' he said. The helicopter had disappeared, although they could still hear its engine. 'I think we'd better get back down and camp for the night,' he continued.

'And tomorrow? What will we do then?' Judy asked.

'When we were coming down in the plane, I saw some smoke to the west,' he said. 'It's worth checking.'

'It might be a campfire,' Judy said hopefully.

'Maybe. There could be a sheep farm out that way. We'll start walking in the morning. It's all we can do, I think.'

He hung the binoculars around his neck and they started back down the hillside to make camp for the night.

Chapter 10 *Brumbies*

The night was cool and there was no moon. It was lucky that Don always carried a torch in his flight case. It was small, but it helped Don and Judy to make a circle of rocks and start a fire inside it. They opened two cans of beans and heated them directly on the fire. They found flat sticks they could use as spoons.

'These beans taste OK,' Judy said, eating a mouthful.

'Yes,' Don replied, 'but we haven't got many cans.'

'Well, as long as we have water, we can probably live quite well,' Judy said. 'There are fish in the creeks, and wild nuts and plants if you know where to look. I've learned quite a bit from living on the farm. People lived here for thousands of years without supermarket food, you know, Dad!'

Don was pleased that his daughter seemed be recovering from her earlier shock.

'You're tired. Get some sleep,' he said.

Judy lay down, resting her head on her backpack, and was soon asleep.

Don sat and looked into the fire, thinking about what had happened. OK, Paul had made a mistake, but he hadn't been thinking of himself. The idea of the flying school had been to bring Don and his family back together and he had paid for his efforts with his life. Then Don looked at Judy. While he was away she had grown into a strong clever girl, and Don was proud of her.

He lay back and looked up at the sky. In the clear night

it was full of stars. He realised he still loved Sylvia and, thanks to Paul, he might now have another chance. If he and Judy got out of here, he told himself, he would tell Sylvia how stupid he had been. He would ask her if they could try again. At last he fell asleep next to his daughter.

* * *

Judy woke in the dawn, stiff and uncomfortable. Her father was still fast asleep. She decided to take the binoculars and climb up the hillside a little way. She could exercise her stiff legs and have a look around. Her father said he had seen smoke the day before, and smoke usually meant people.

After ten minutes, she stopped. The sun was just coming up over the top of the hill. She turned and looked back down the valley, and saw some moving shapes by the creek. At first she thought the kangaroos had come back, but these animals didn't jump like kangaroos as they moved. Through the binoculars she saw they were horses drinking at the creek. 'Brumbies,' she thought. 'Free, wild horses.'

She had an idea: maybe they could use them. Thanks to Patrick Forsha she knew how to ride, and she was sure her father had some experience. Her own horse had been quite wild at first, but she had controlled the animal with patience.

Judy went quickly back down the hillside. Her father was awake now. He was building the fire again.

'Where have you been? I was worried,' he said.

'Dad, I saw some brumbies down the valley!' Judy said excitedly.

Don looked up. 'Brumbies? I didn't think there were wild horses in this part of the country,' he said. 'I know there are thousands further south, in the Snowy Mountains.'

'Well, some of them must have wandered north,' Judy said. 'We can ride them, Dad! We'll be able to travel much more quickly.'

'Judy, brumbies are *wild* horses. We might not be able to get near them,' Don said. However, Judy was confident.

'My horse Sasha was difficult at first. I had a battle with her, but I stayed on. It didn't take that long. I'm not frightened of horses, Dad. I know how to handle them.'

In the end, Don agreed it was worth a try. He was worried, but it was a chance. Inside he felt pleased that Judy was the kind of girl who was willing to take a risk.

After a breakfast of more beans they collected their things together and walked back towards the place where Judy had seen the horses. There were about eight brumbies drinking at the edge of the creek. Some of them moved away as Don and Judy approached.

'Can I have your knife, Dad, and the rope?'

Don took the thin rope off his shoulder and passed her the knife. She cut two equal lengths of rope and tied knots in each piece so that it made a ring big enough to put over the neck of a horse and left some rope for them to hold on to. Then she quietly moved towards the brumbies. When she was three meters away from the nearest, she threw the rope. The rope went over the brumby's head and it jumped and kicked immediately. Don joined Judy, helping her to hold onto the rope. The horse tried to get away, pulling both of them over and dragging them along the ground a little way, until Don managed to tie the end of the rope round a nearby tree. The brumby kicked for a while, but soon calmed down. Some of the other brumbies slowly wandered back and started drinking and chewing the dry grass again.

'OK, I'm going to get on,' said Judy.

'Be careful,' said her father.

Judy calmly walked up to the horse. She knew that confidence was important. She had to believe that she was in charge. If Judy believed it, the brumby would believe it.

'Untie the rope now, Dad.'

Don watched, amazed and proud at how his daughter handled the horse. She held tightly onto the rope, though the brumby sometimes jumped. At last the horse walked calmly around as Judy pulled the rope to the left or the right.

'Nothing to sit on, but we'll have to manage,' said Judy. Smiling, she got down and tied the horse up once more. 'Now for the next one.'

The next brumby took a little longer. When Judy had it under control, she held the rope while Don got on carefully. He hadn't ridden a horse for many years, and he felt stiff and uncomfortable on the animal's back.

It was around eleven in the morning. They had spent two hours trying to control the brumbies. 'We're ready, I think,' said Judy.

'We'll head west, in the direction I saw the smoke yesterday. Let's hope there are people there,' Don said. 'We should give these horses names. They're both females. How about Daphne and Chloe?'

'Too old-fashioned! Let's call them Kylie and Nicole. You've got Nicole – Kylie's smaller.'

Don laughed. 'OK, Kylie and Nicole they are. You're the boss.' They set off towards the west.

Chapter 11 *Breaking news*

On the same evening that the *Sugar Glider* crashed, Sylvia got up and walked to the balcony of her large comfortable room at the new Prima Hotel on the Gold Coast. Patrick's hotel had only opened the week before; it was a modern white building, twenty storeys high. She stood and looked down on the wide beaches of the northern Gold Coast. The television in the room was on, but out here the soft noises of the sea below came to her. Patrick was at another business meeting.

Sylvia thought about him, and wondered if she had done the right thing, coming to the hotel. The day had been pleasant. They had eaten a relaxing late lunch with champagne at a seafood restaurant, and then gone for a walk along the beach. They had seen a Japanese couple getting married on the beautiful white sands, a wedding right next to the sea.

'I love that about this country,' Patrick had said. 'People can get married anywhere. On a river, on the top of a mountain . . .'

Sylvia had tried to change the subject. She didn't want to talk about people getting married. But Patrick had kept on talking about his and Sylvia's relationship. He wanted her to move back to the city. He had an apartment she and Judy could live in, he said. Sylvia had stayed quiet.

She was glad he had gone to the meeting. He had apologised and told her to enjoy the hotel. Actually, she was happy to have time to herself. It was good for her and Judy to have a break from each other too, she thought. That didn't happen often when there was no father around. But would Patrick be any sort of father to Judy? He tried to be kind, but Sylvia worried that he didn't really understand children. She also felt that Judy didn't like him.

And Don coming back had changed things. She had thought it was over between them, but seeing him again had brought back old feelings. She often wondered what had really caused them to break up. Perhaps she had been selfish. There had been plenty of good times too, before the fights.

On the television the evening news began. In Australia the season of storms and bush fires had started. She decided to go in and call Judy at the Copemans' house.

Beulah answered. 'Sylvia? Thank God you called. I had no idea where you were.'

'Why, what's wrong?' Sylvia said, her heart beating faster.

'Paul hasn't rung. They should have been in Melbourne two hours ago, but when I rang the museum they still hadn't arrived.'

'It's not that long,' Sylvia said. 'They might have left late.'

'They didn't. I checked with the airfield.'

'Is Judy worried, Beulah? Can I speak to her?'

'Judy? Sylvia, what do you mean? Judy went with them,' Beulah said.

'What?' Sylvia felt sick.

'Didn't you know?'

'I had no idea.' Sylvia's legs went weak. She sat on the sofa in front of the television.

'I suppose it happened at the last minute. I think Don

felt bad about leaving Judy behind. She was really excited about the trip. It was such an adventure for her. I just thought Don or Judy would have called to tell you.' Beulah was crying.

'Have they started a search?' Sylvia asked.

'It's dark now. Air Rescue has got the flight plan from Everett's Field, and they'll start looking first thing in the morning. I've got their number.'

'Give it to me, please.' Sylvia wrote it down quickly. 'Thanks Beulah. Let's try and keep calm. We'll keep in touch tomorrow.' She gave Beulah her mobile number and rang off.

Sylvia got up and walked around the room. She mustn't panic. On the news they were talking about something happening at a mine in Queensland, but she was hardly listening. 'Don and Paul are very experienced pilots,' she said to herself. 'They wouldn't put themselves and Judy in danger. It got dark, so they've probably landed somewhere else, for safety. It's too soon to think the worst.'

She sat down again in front of the television. She wanted to think about something else. There were pictures of people singing and shouting. A man was speaking about the government's broken promises. Then the camera moved around the crowd.

Sylvia's mouth fell open. There on the television, was her daughter. Judy was sitting on a rock, reading a magazine. Where was this place? When had she been there? From the light, it looked like early afternoon. The picture changed. Now they were talking about bush fires in Western Australia. She reached for her phone and dialled the number Beulah had given her.

A woman answered. Sylvia's voice was shaking. 'It's about a missing plane.'

'Wait one minute please.' A few seconds, then a man's voice came on the phone.

'This is Richard Heron, operations control. I'm sorry Mrs . . .?'

'Radcliffe. My ex-husband is (she didn't want to say *was*) one of the pilots on the plane that's gone missing between Everett's Field near Brisbane, and Melbourne. And my daughter is a passenger.'

'I see. The *Sugar Glider*. I'm very sorry, you must be very worried, but I'm afraid there's nothing we can do until it's light. We'll start first thing in the morning. We have a team ready,' the man replied.

'But I just saw my daughter on TV. It was on the news. It was a mine somewhere in Queensland. There was a demonstration there or something.'

'What channel was the news on?'

Sylvia looked at the television. 'Channel nine.'

'Just a minute. Please hold the line.'

Sylvia waited, for a long time it seemed. At last Heron came back to the phone. 'I've just checked. The demonstration was in Warrangi, in Queensland, but the plane wasn't going there. We have their flight plan which shows their route, and it goes nowhere near Warrangi. Are you sure?'

'I know what my daughter looks like,' Sylvia said angrily.

'All right. It's strange, but we'll work with this information. Please give me your number. We'll keep you up to date. Try not to worry too much.'

'Thank you.' Sylvia hung up. Immediately, she dialled

Patrick's mobile number. He answered rather crossly, 'Yes, what is it?'

'It's Sylvia. Something has happened. Judy – '

Forsha interrupted her. 'Oh Sylvia. I'm sorry, but I've got a bit of a problem here. I'll call you back in five minutes.'

Sylvia went back to the balcony. The noise of the sea calmed her a little. She was trying not to cry. Patrick was a busy man, of course. In the end he might have even less time for her than Don had had.

Five minutes later the telephone rang, making her jump.

'Sylvia?' It was Patrick. 'I'm sorry, a few problems here. My accountants are giving me a headache.' He was speaking very quickly. 'Now, what's happened?'

'Patrick, Judy went on a plane to Melbourne with Don and it's gone missing.'

'What? What do you mean she went on that plane with Don?' Patrick was almost shouting.

'She was going to stay in Brisbane with Paul's wife – Paul's the other pilot – until they got back. She didn't tell me.'

'Oh God. I'm so sorry, Sylvia. You must be worried sick. But keep calm. It may not be the worst yet. I'm sure the authorities are doing all they can. They usually find missing planes, even in a country as big as this, and the *Sugar Glider*'s a big plane. Look, I'll be finished here soon and then I'll be back as quickly as I can.'

'Patrick, if you don't mind, I want to be alone tonight.'

'Sylvia – '

'Please, Patrick.'

'Well, all right. I'll make some calls too, and try and find out what I can. I'll call you back if I hear something, OK? See you in the morning.'

'All right, Patrick. Thank you.' Sylvia hung up. She needed to walk, to clear her head. She went downstairs, left the hotel and walked along the beach. The night was full of stars.

'It's my fault,' she thought. 'I was angry with Don for leaving her behind, so he took her. I wish I hadn't come here.'

She felt frightened. 'Don, what's happened?' she said to herself. 'Please be all right. I don't want to lose both of you.'

Chapter 12 *Accident*

By one o'clock in the afternoon Judy and Don were hot and tired. The landscape they were riding through was becoming flatter. They stopped to rest by a creek full of small fish. Judy surprised Don by making a simple fish trap and catching two fish. They made a fire and cooked the fish in it.

'You've learned a lot, living out in the country,' said Don.

Judy smiled. 'I missed Brisbane at first, but there's a lot of nice things about living on the land,' she said. 'I feel very free there.'

Don looked at her. 'Judy, I want to tell you I'm sorry.'

'It's OK, Dad.' Judy looked straight into the fire.

'No, I'm sorry for everything,' he went on. 'Not just for getting you into this mess. I wish I'd never left you and your mother either.'

'Really?'

'Yes, really.'

'I wish you'd never left, too,' she said sadly.

Don continued, 'I don't really know why I did. My job was everything to me, but it was hurting your mother. I was away a lot, and when I was home I was tired. It seemed neither of us could be happy. Flying means freedom to me. I kept my freedom, but I hurt you and your mother. I want to put things right, if it's not too late.'

Judy went to her father and kissed him. 'I forgive you.

You'll have to talk to Mum, though,' Judy said. 'If we get back.'

'We will. And you're a very brave girl. I'm proud of you,' said Don.

They finished their meal and rode on. The land was turning yellow-brown. It hadn't rained here for some time. Riding without anything to sit on was making both of them sore. They came to the top of another valley, and flat land lay below them.

'It's grassland,' said Judy, looking through her binoculars. 'I think I can see a fence in the distance.' She passed the binoculars to her father.

'You may be right,' her father answered. 'It could be a sheep station, but let's not get too excited. Sheep stations can be huge out here. We could still be far from help.'

Don felt tired and angry with himself. His whole body ached. 'Well, let's just keep on. We'll find somewhere.'

Suddenly a bird flew out of a tree. Surprised, Don kicked his horse's sides, and Nicole jumped and started to run. Don held on for a while, but Nicole shook her head and the rope flew out of Don's hand. He held on desperately to the horse's neck. Nicole jumped to one side, and Don came off, rolling down the hill they had just climbed. He landed on a flat piece of rock with a steep drop below him.

'Dad, Dad!' Judy shouted. She jumped off Kylie and ran down the hill after him. Don was lying on his back. His right leg was bent under him, but his eyes were open.

'Dad! Can you move?' Judy cried.

Don lifted his head and groaned. 'I think my leg's broken! It hurts . . .'

Then his head fell back and his eyes closed. 'Dad! Dad!' Judy cried, feeling panic coming. She fought to control it. What could she do now? Was this the end for both of them? Would they die out here, in this big empty land?

She breathed deeply, and tried to think clearly. She had to go on and get help. First she made her father as comfortable as she could. His backpack had come off in the fall. She went back to fetch it, so she could use it as a pillow for him. He was in the sun, but she didn't dare move his leg, even if she could drag him. Her father was a big man. She took out her water bottle. His eyes opened when she poured water into his mouth.

'Dad?' He nodded. 'I'll have to go on and look for help. It's our only chance,' she said.

Don looked at her. 'You're right,' he said, in a voice filled with pain.

Judy went on, 'Since that helicopter we haven't seen one plane, friendly or otherwise. I don't understand it. The authorities must be looking for us by now, surely.'

'It's a big area to search,' Don said, knowing that if they were going to be safe, he and Judy had to find help themselves.

Judy kissed her father. 'I'll be back with help, I promise.' She was trying not to cry.

'Go quickly. I'll be fine,' Don said.

Judy had to find her horse. Nicole had disappeared, but she found Kylie nearby, calmly eating grass. 'What luck,' she said to herself. She climbed onto the horse's back and set off down the other side of the valley towards the endless flat land.

'This is such a big country,' she thought. She could

imagine what it had been like for the first British explorers, coming from a small, cold country. They must have been amazed. No wonder people stayed near the coast, where all the cities are today.

Then she thought about people like the Murri. Some of them still walked all over the country. They still knew how to read the land; they saw things in it that most people could not see. They had a different idea about the land. It was a living thing to them, something to care for.

Her thoughts came back to the present. She knew that the people who had damaged the plane and forced it down were dangerous. Whoever they were, they wanted the uranium, and she knew it was worth millions. Because of the uranium Paul was dead and her father was lying injured in the bush. She knew she had to keep going.

After riding for an hour she stopped by a single black tree. She was scared of getting lost, but she pushed the fear away. She put the water bottle to her lips and drank, looking at the land ahead. There was a small group of trees in the distance. She rode on until she came to the trees. Near them was a small pool of water, a drinking hole for animals. She tasted the water. It was quite clean. She filled her bottle gratefully and sat in the welcome shade. She started to feel better.

After a short rest, she got back on Kylie and continued her journey, stopping only to look through the binoculars from time to time. The third or fourth time she looked, she noticed something in the distance, where the land met the sky. It was moving and was made of something shiny, metal maybe. Excited, she rode on. In a few minutes she could see what it was: a windmill, turning gently in the wind. Out here, windmills were used to draw water from the ground. 'There must be people near!' she thought and pushed Kylie on towards the windmill.

Chapter 13 *Tarong station*

After another twenty minutes she came to a dirt road. 'A road must lead somewhere,' she said to herself with growing excitement. It was not long before she saw a wooden farmhouse in the distance, shining white in the afternoon sun. There were two vehicles nearby, an open truck and an old car.

She got down and tied Kylie to a gatepost, then she walked up to the house. At last she could get help. Judy looked at her watch. It was five o'clock. She had left her father three hours ago. There wasn't much of the day left.

She walked up the front steps to the outside deck. Some wooden chairs and a table stood at the side of an open door. The sound of a radio came from somewhere inside, playing country music.

'Is anyone at home?' she called out. There was no answer. Softly, she walked through the door. 'Is anyone there?' she called again. She followed the sound of the radio to a large kitchen. The smell of food suddenly reminded her that she was hungry.

A voice behind her interrupted her thoughts, making her jump.

'Hello. I didn't realise I had a visitor.'

Judy turned round. At the open door there was a tall man with a sunburned face and grey hair. He held a wide brown hat in his hand.

'Thank goodness.' Judy's words rushed out

uncontrollably. 'Please, my father – he's in danger. We crashed. The *Sugar Glider* –'

'Just a minute, young lady. Slow down. First of all, who are you?' the man said.

'I'm sorry. I'm Judy Radcliffe.'

'And I'm John Fittock and this is my sheep station you've found, Tarong. You look like you've had a bit of a journey.'

Judy saw herself in a kitchen mirror. Her hair was wild and unbrushed, and her face was burned. There was dust and dirt all over her clothes. She started to cry.

'Come here and sit down,' Fittock said, 'and tell me from the beginning.'

Judy took a deep breath. 'I was on my way to Melbourne in an old plane, the *Sugar Glider.* My father and his friend were flying it, but we crashed yesterday, and Paul, my dad's friend, was killed.' She stopped, remembering what had happened to Paul. Her body started shaking. Fittock put his hand on her shoulder.

'Take it easy, girl. Where's your father?'

'After we left the plane we found some brumbies and rode them, but my father fell off. I think he's broken his leg. Please, we have to get help,' Judy said.

John whistled. 'So you were in a plane crash; you're still alive; you found wild horses and managed to ride them. That's quite something! When did you come down exactly?'

'Yesterday evening,' Judy answered. 'We camped near the plane for the night. We found the brumbies this morning.'

'And you've been travelling since then? Well, you look

like you need some food. Why don't you have a shower while I organise something for you?'

'Please, you must call someone!' Judy begged.

'I will, don't worry. You're safe now. Just relax. I'll show you the bathroom.'

Judy accepted gratefully. She felt better as soon as the shower water touched her. As she was drying herself she heard John's voice, somewhere in the house. 'He must be calling Air Rescue,' she thought. She hoped they could find her father before it got dark.

When she returned to the kitchen John had prepared steak, eggs and bread. At that moment it seemed the best meal she had ever tasted.

'Do you live here alone?' Judy asked as she was finishing her food.

'My wife's visiting our son in Sydney,' John said. 'And most of our workers are on their way back from Queensland. I've got some Murri people working for me here. They went up to demonstrate about land rights, at a mine I think. They're from a group that came from Warrangi originally.'

'Warrangi?' Judy was surprised. 'How far is that?'

'About a day's drive.'

'We stopped there before we crashed!' Judy said.

'Yes, I know,' said John. 'Some men told us when they came earlier today, looking for you.'

'What men?' asked Judy, her eyes opening wide.

'They said they were from the government. I just called them. You'll be all right, don't worry. They're on their way now. We'll soon get your dad and you'll be home before you know it.'

Judy didn't like it. Something wasn't right. 'Can I call my mother?' she said.

'Sure. The phone's in the back of the house.' He stopped as a loud noise filled the sky above them.

'Must be the government people. They don't waste any time,' said Fittock. 'We'd better go and meet them.'

Judy followed him to the front of the house, her heart starting to beat fast. A helicopter was landing fifty meters away. Judy's stomach sank when she saw it was the same one she had seen with her father the day before in the valley. There were three men inside. Judy could see a face she thought she recognised. It looked like the face of the tall thin mechanic she had seen at Warrangi driving the refuelling truck for the *Sugar Glider*.

Chapter 14 *Prisoners*

Judy backed away as the three men came up the steps of the house. She wanted to look for a phone, quickly. The thin man seemed to be the leader. When he saw John at the door, he said in a hard voice, 'Where's the girl?'

'She's here, she . . .' He turned round. 'She must have gone back inside. She's had a rough time.'

The three men pushed past him and entered the house. They found Judy standing against the wall at the back of the house, a phone in her hand. The thin man grabbed it from her hand.

'Judy Radcliffe?' he said.

Judy nodded, her face white. 'Who are you?'

'Carl Petersen. Where's the plane you came in? We need to find it, and quickly.'

'Where are the pilots, Copeman and Radcliffe?' said another man.

'Paul Copeman is dead. He had a heart attack when we came down. Then my father had an accident in the bush. I think his leg is broken. Please, we have to get to him. We –'

'All in good time,' Petersen interrupted. 'We need you to take us to the plane, quickly. It's called the *Sugar Glider*, isn't it? Did it glide?' He smiled, but it was not a friendly smile.

Judy thought fast. Now she was sure the men didn't work for the government.

'I'll help you after we rescue my father,' Judy said, a determined look in her eye.

Petersen looked at her coldly. 'I don't think you realise how serious this is.' He grabbed her shoulder and pushed her along the corridor and into the kitchen. The other two men came in with John. One was carrying a machine gun. Judy was shaking inside, but she answered firmly.

'It's very serious,' she said. 'My father's out in the bush with a broken leg and very little food and water. I'll help you find the plane when he's safe.'

Petersen stared at Judy. Judy stared back. One of the other men spoke. 'Maybe we don't need her. Fittock told us which direction she came from and how many hours she must have been travelling. We can work out where the plane is.'

Petersen thought for a moment. 'You could be right. Put them both in a room and lock the door. I'm going out to the helicopter. I have to call the boss on the radio.'

One of the men waved his gun at Judy and John. 'Where are the keys to the rooms?' he said.

John pointed at some keys hanging on a hook by the door. The man picked them up and told them to move. John and Judy left the kitchen and went back down the corridor. The man behind them kept his gun ready.

They came to a door on the left. 'In there,' the man said. It was a small room with a bed, a desk, a cupboard and two chairs. When Judy and John were inside, the door shut hard. They heard a key turn.

'Government people don't carry machine guns!' said Judy.

'No, they don't,' John said, a worried look on his face.

'What are we going to do?' Judy asked. It was turning into a nightmare.

'You might have to do as they say,' John replied. 'They mean business. It could be the only way to help your father. Why don't you take them to the plane? Then they'll leave us alone,' he said, but he sounded uncertain.

'They're prepared to leave my father out there to die. They might just kill me too, if I take them to the plane. There's something else I didn't tell you.'

'What?' John asked.

'The plane was carrying uranium.'

John's eyes opened wide.

Judy went on. 'None of us knew it before. I think Paul, the other pilot, found out when we got to the mine, but he didn't tell us. Then they did something to the plane, to force us to land soon after we left. But my dad changed course, so we didn't come down where they expected to find us. Otherwise I think we'd all be dead already.'

'I made a mistake calling those people. I didn't know,' said John.

A few minutes later, they heard Petersen coming back towards the house. He began talking to the other two outside. Judy put her ear to the door. She could hear only parts of the conversation.

'. . . must be in the area . . . Mr F said . . . the pilot doesn't matter . . . make it look like an accident . . . get the stuff at all costs . . . don't touch the girl . . . keep her at the station . . . wait until the business is finished.'

'We've got to get to my dad,' whispered Judy.

They heard the helicopter's engines starting. Judy went to the window. The helicopter was lifting off, with Petersen and another man inside. The third man had stayed behind to guard Judy and John.

An hour passed. It was getting dark now, and it felt cooler in the room. The only noise came from a couple of flies at the window. John looked silently out of the window. Judy thought about her father. She had left him water, but he would need more. He might be cold in the night, but she was helpless to do anything. How long could he stay alive out there?

Suddenly there was a tapping sound from under the floor. 'What's that?' Judy said.

John said nothing, but smiled and got down on the floor. He moved his hands over the carpet, as if feeling for something. He found a cut edge, and lifted part of the carpet away from the floor. There were wooden boards underneath, and some of these were cut also. John pushed at one end and the boards moved.

'It's a door,' John said in a low voice, 'a trapdoor. Something I made for the kids when they were small! Only me and a couple of my workers know about it. We never use it now because it isn't safe.'

As Judy looked in wonder, a head appeared covered with black wavy hair. A face turned up towards them. Judy's eyes opened even wider as she recognised the boy she had spoken with at Warrangi. That seemed like a lifetime ago.

* * *

Back on the lonely hillside, Don Radcliffe could see that the sun was getting lower in the sky. His leg ached terribly. Judy must have got lost, he thought. He tried not to sink into hopelessness. All of his plans seemed like dreams now.

He still wanted more than anything to bring his family back together, to make a new start, but he had to accept that he might never see them again. 'Judy, Sylvia, I'm sorry.' He groaned bitterly.

He was starting to feel hot and faint. 'I've got no more water,' he thought. He thought about how many explorers had died in Australia's history, because of the climate and the size of the place. Coming from the green lands of Europe to this burnt brown land, how could they have been prepared?

He fell into a light sleep and began to have a strange dream. The *Sugar Glider* changed into the odd animal that had given the plane its name. He heard its yip-yip-yip call. It seemed to be laughing at him. Then it was a plane again. He heard its engines above him.

He woke up. The noise of engines was real, but it wasn't from a plane, the noise was coming from a helicopter. He recognised the sound. It was the same helicopter they had heard that morning at the creek. 'Not rescuers,' he thought. 'They'll see me here; I've got to get away.' Painfully, he pulled himself towards the edge of the rock. He could see some bushes on the hillside, a few meters away. If he could just get to them, he'd be hidden. He managed to reach the edge of the rock. A branch was sticking out of the hillside. He reached out with both hands, but when he pulled, it came away in the loose earth. Then he felt himself falling again.

Chapter 15 *Playing for time*

The boy climbed into the room and John dropped the boards quietly back into place. 'Hello Joe,' whispered John. 'You never liked using the front door, did you?'

'I didn't like your guests much, those guys in the helicopter,' said Joe.

'Meet Joe, Judy,' John Fittock said. 'He works for me; one of my best young men.'

'We've met. You're a long way from Warrangi, eh?' Joe said in a low voice, smiling at Judy. 'But I knew you were here, anyway.'

'How?' said Judy, surprised.

'Your shoes. You left marks all around the place.'

'Joe can see more than most people.' John grinned. 'Glad you remembered the trapdoor. You've come at the right time, Joe.'

'Yeah,' Joe said. 'We were on our way back from Warrangi when we saw the helicopter coming down here and the men with guns. We thought it was safe when the helicopter went away again but they left one man here. He's asleep at the moment. What's going on?'

Judy told him what had happened.

'So,' said Joe when she had finished, 'there's uranium at Warrangi. They kept that quiet.' Joe's face was angry. 'Warrangi's a very special place to us.'

'Why is it so special?' Judy was curious.

'We have to protect it,' said Joe. 'It's part of our history.

Everything in the land comes from the Dreamtime, a time before history began. Every living thing has its own dreaming place. White people don't understand. Probably never will.'

There was a noise from outside. The man guarding them was moving around. The three of them froze. After a moment they could hear the noise of a chair as he sat down again.

'These men are killers.' Judy spoke more quietly. 'They'll kill my father if they find him, maybe all of us, when they have what they want. We have to get to my father.'

'That's no problem,' Joe said. 'I can find the way, but I'll have to wait till first light.'

'They want her to show them where the plane came down,' John said. 'They've gone off looking for it now, but I don't think they'll find it today. Look, Judy, I've got an idea. When they come back, why don't you tell them you'll do it. It's dark now, so they'll have to wait till tomorrow.'

'You mean we have to stay here tonight?' Judy was frightened.

'Yeah, it's our best chance,' John replied. 'Try and keep them waiting tomorrow – act sick, show them the wrong place. Anything to give Joe time to get to your dad.'

'And Joe, tell the police, the army, anyone. If the wrong people get the uranium, terrorists maybe, it could be awful. There's a radio in your brother's truck, isn't there?'

'Yeah, but it doesn't work properly. We've tried to fix it, but it's no good. My brother's waiting for me out there. I'd better get going.' Joe looked at Judy. 'Don't worry. We'll get to your dad before those guys do.' To John, he said,

'Have you got any clothes in this room – men's clothes?'

'This was my son's room. Some of his stuff is in that cupboard. Help yourself. What do you want clothes for?' John asked.

'Just an idea,' Joe said. He opened the cupboard, chose a few clothes and put them into a plastic bag. Then he opened the trapdoor in the floor and started to climb down. Before he disappeared completely, Judy asked him. 'What dreaming place is Warrangi?'

He looked at her. 'It's the sugar glider dreaming place. I'll tell you the story some time.' Judy opened her mouth in surprise. Then Joe was gone.

Twenty minutes later the helicopter came back. They heard Petersen and his men outside.

'We'll just have to try again in the morning,' one of them was saying angrily.

'I'll start pretending to feel sick,' said Judy. 'Call them.' John knocked loudly on the door of the room. Judy lay down on the bed. In a few moments the door opened. Petersen was standing there with an angry expression.

'Look, she's really worried about her dad,' said the farmer.

'She knows what to do if she wants to see him,' said Petersen.

'She's feeling sick now, but she says she'll help you find the plane in the morning, if she's well enough.'

'She'd better be,' said Petersen.

Chapter 16 *The search*

Judy woke at dawn. She could hear the noise of people moving about. John Fittock was allowed to bring her some tea.

'They want to get away early,' he told her.

'Tell them I'm still feeling sick,' she said, hoping that Joe was on his way to her dad. If he were on foot, he would need a lot of time. Judy stayed in the bathroom for an hour, pretending to be sick. Finally, Petersen banged on the door.

'We're going right now,' he said. When she came out, he held her arm tightly and led her out of the house towards the helicopter. She noticed that Kylie had gone. Either she had escaped, or Joe had taken her. Petersen pushed her into the seat next to the pilot, and got in behind her. The same guard stayed behind with John.

The pilot spoke to Petersen. 'I thought you said the boss told us to keep the girl at Tarong?'

'We've got to find the plane. Just fly,' Petersen answered. As the helicopter rose sharply, Judy felt her stomach drop. She had never flown in a helicopter before.

The farmhouse below became smaller, and they turned away, in the direction she had come from on Kylie the day before. She looked back. There was an empty seat next to Petersen, and some space behind. There was a large metal net, to carry the uranium she supposed. There was also some equipment for cutting metal, and a box with the word 'Explosives' in large black letters on the top.

'You look outside,' Petersen shouted, 'and follow the route.' Judy looked out. They were flying over the first gentle hills.

'I came along that way, I think,' she said, pointing along a valley. Petersen ordered the pilot to turn. 'We crashed into some trees, and they covered the plane. This valley looks familiar. Yes, we're near.'

In fact, she had no idea where they were. She only wanted to waste as much time as possible, to buy time for Joe, or for rescuers.

'Put us down there,' Petersen told the pilot. They landed in a small clearing.

Judy led them along the valley, past a creek she had never seen before. It was hotter than the day before, and they all began to sweat in the heat. Flies were all around them.

Finally, Judy said, 'I'm sorry. I thought this was the place but it's not. This area all looks the same.' Petersen looked at her sharply. They went back to the helicopter and took off again.

They landed twice more. Each time they walked around the bush, but found nothing. They were all tired and hot. Petersen was becoming very angry.

'You're messing us around, girl,' he said coldly.

'I'm sorry. I'm trying but I'm confused. It was all such a shock.'

'Then try harder,' Petersen said. 'Remember your father. How long do you want him to stay out here – if he's still alive?'

'I am trying,' she said, fighting back the tears.

Another hour passed.

'She can't have come from this far,' said the pilot. 'I'm turning round.'

They flew low, heading back now in the direction of Tarong. Judy began to recognise the landscape. She saw the spot where they had found the brumbies. Soon she saw the place where Don had fallen off Nicole, and the rock where she had left him. She went pale when she saw there was no one there. Had Joe found her father?

Petersen saw the expression on her face. He told the pilot to go lower.

'You were here, weren't you? Is this where your father fell?' Judy said nothing.

The helicopter went down. The pilot pointed. 'Look!' They saw a figure far below, on the valley floor. Petersen picked up his machine gun. Judy looked down, terrified.

'Looks like he tried to get off the rock, and fell. Shall I go down?' said the pilot.

'Don't bother. No one could be alive after a fall like that,' said Petersen. 'I'm sorry, girl.' To the pilot, he said, 'At least he's saved us the trouble.'

So Joe's journey had been useless after all. Judy could not stop her tears now.

They followed the valley back, away from Tarong.

'You must have come this way,' Petersen said, but Judy didn't answer. 'Look there. Looks like the remains of a fire.'

Through her tears, Judy saw the place she had camped with her father, that first night.

'I'll go down,' said the pilot. They landed near the circle of rocks that she and Don had made.

'So you camped here!' Petersen said. 'Now you must know where the plane is. Don't waste any more of my time.'

She led them to the *Sugar Glider* in silence. There was no point in wasting any more time. She was too late to help her father now.

'Check inside,' Petersen told the helicopter pilot, who climbed in through the bottom of the plane. A few minutes later he reappeared.

'It's all still here. The pilot's dead, as the girl said. The stuff is difficult to get at, though. We'll need to cut a hole in the roof.'

'OK. I'll radio the boss and tell him we've found it.'

'He'll be pleased,' said the pilot. 'I heard he was having a few money problems. Too much building – '

'Shut up,' said Petersen.

'You're not from the government, are you?' said Judy, through her tears. 'What are you going to do with the uranium?'

Petersen looked at Judy for a long moment. 'I suppose it doesn't matter if we tell you. We're going to sell it, that's all. To the ones who've got the most money. We've got a buyer.'

He switched on the helicopter radio. 'I'd better call the boss,' he said. 'I want to finish this business. Start getting the equipment out.'

Chapter 17 *Taking care of business*

A thin man with thick blond hair walked into the embassy building in Canberra. The secretary told him to go straight up to the main office.

'He's been expecting you,' she said.

The blond man walked up the stairs and knocked on a heavy wooden door. An older man with silver hair was sitting in a fine leather chair in a large office. He pressed a button on his phone. 'Do not disturb us,' he said into the phone. The two men spoke together in a foreign language.

'Berjenka,' the silver-haired man said, 'you're still in Australia! I heard the news about the rescue services looking for the missing plane. I was beginning to think the deal was cancelled.'

'Cancelled?' Berjenka replied. 'Not at all. I'm expecting a call this morning to say that the uranium is in our hands. I've come to check that you have the money ready.'

'It has been ready for some time,' the silver-haired man replied. He went to the wall and opened a safe. He took out a black leather case. 'But I think you have been having some difficulties.'

'Difficulties? What do you mean?' Berjenka answered.

'The authorities know that the plane stopped at the mine. I hope they do not also know about the uranium?' the silver-haired man said, raising his eyebrows.

'Are you saying we should cancel the deal?' Berjenka asked.

'If anything goes wrong there could be problems between our country and Australia. You must understand that you are on your own. I know nothing about this matter, nothing. Do you understand?'

'Yes, sir.' Berjenka nodded.

'Go now. I suggest that if nothing happens today, you should leave Australia without the uranium, as soon as possible.'

'Yes, sir.' He turned and walked out of the office. In the street he was about to wave down a taxi when the phone rang in his pocket. It was a familiar voice.

'I have been waiting for your call,' said Berjenka in English. 'I was beginning to think our agreement was off.'

'We've found the plane,' a voice said. 'They changed course and came down in the mountains. The things you want are not damaged.'

'Good,' said Berjenka. 'The pilots?'

'Both pilots are dead.'

'Where is the plane exactly?' Berjenka asked.

'Eastern New South Wales,' the voice on the phone said. 'I'll tell you exactly where when we agree on the details.'

'The "details"? I thought everything was agreed,' Berjenka said, with some surprise in his voice.

'I meant the money.'

'Ah, the money. Of course. But we have already agreed what the amount would be.'

'There have been more costs than I thought,' the voice said.

'That is not my fault. Anyway, I do not think you are in a good position to make demands,' Berjenka said.

'What do you mean?'

'We know about your business problems,' Berjenka said. 'You have made bad decisions, and you owe money. You need the money to save your companies, and now your government is looking for the plane also. The amount of money will stay the same, or we cannot do business.'

'There are other customers. Others are interested.'

'I do not believe you.' There was silence from the telephone. 'And in any case, neither of us has much time,' Berjenka added.

The voice on the other end of the telephone paused. Finally, it said, 'All right. I hope you have plans to get it out of the country immediately?'

'Yes, of course. I have a plane ready.'

'Meet me at this place.' The voice gave Berjenka some numbers, so that the place could be found on a map. 'From there we'll have to go in my helicopter.'

'A helicopter? Why?' Berjenka asked.

'The plane crashed in the mountains. Only a helicopter can land there. We'll have to take the uranium back to your plane.'

'In that case you will only get your money when the materials are safe on my plane,' Berjenka said angrily.

'How soon can you get there?'

'Two or three hours, I think. I am on my way now. Nothing must go wrong.' Berjenka hung up, then he called his men. The plane would be ready in twenty minutes.

Chapter 18 *The meeting point*

Judy sat down on a rock and put her head in her hands. She wondered what would happen to her, now these people had what they wanted. Could she escape? They had guns, and she was still tired from the travelling of the day before. One of them was always watching her, even when they were working. And where could she go?

She felt something hard in her pocket. It was the perfume bottle pressing against her leg. Her dad had said she might use it one day, but it was impossible to imagine that now. She watched Petersen and the pilot cut a hole in the roof of the *Sugar Glider*. Then they lifted the uranium out using the helicopter, and put it on the ground about five hundred meters away. The operation took less than half an hour.

When they were finished, Petersen said, 'I think we'd better blow up the plane. It'll remove all the evidence. Bring the explosives. The jet fuel in the tanks will do the rest.'

Petersen went into the plane to lay the explosives. The pilot followed him in. For a moment, no one was watching Judy.

'This could be my only chance,' she thought.

She got up slowly. Out of the corner of her eye, Judy saw someone come out of the bush. It was a man carrying a small white bag and moving silently towards the helicopter. He had something else in his hand. It looked like a piece of thin metal.

Judy suddenly recognised the figure. It was Joe, and he was doing something to the helicopter's fuel tank. He looked up and smiled at Judy. Then he put his finger to his lips. Judy nodded and looked back towards the *Sugar Glider*. The men were coming out of the plane.

'OK, let's get away from the plane,' Petersen said. They all moved back towards the helicopter. When Judy turned round, Joe had gone.

'Ready?' Petersen said. He had a small box in his hand, with a button on it. Just at that moment there was a noise in the sky. Another helicopter was coming down towards them.

'Wait, it's the boss,' the pilot said.

Petersen put down the box. The helicopter landed about fifty meters from Petersen's larger machine. Two men got out. One was thin, with thick blond hair. The other was a tall man with shiny black hair. Judy's eyes opened wide as she realised who it was. Patrick! 'Has he come to rescue me?' she asked herself. She called his name.

Patrick Forsha turned and saw her and his expression changed to horror. 'What's she doing here?' he said angrily to Petersen, when he reached them. 'I told you to keep her at Tarong!'

'We were trying to save time, boss. The authorities might be getting closer.'

'What is this, Mr Forsha? Who is this girl?' said the blond man.

Judy was shocked. Patrick was their boss? What did he have to do with the plane crash and the uranium? She didn't understand.

'It doesn't matter, Berjenka. As you can see, the uranium

is here. We can take it to your plane, and then you can give us the money.'

There was a noise in the bush. 'What's that?' Patrick turned around. A horse ran out of the bush. Judy saw it was Kylie, the horse she had ridden all the way to Tarong!

'It's just a brumby,' said Petersen's pilot.

'Something frightened it, or someone. Go and look,' Patrick said. Petersen and the pilot went off towards the trees, guns ready.

'Mr Forsha, we do not have much time,' Berjenka began.

Suddenly a shot rang out. A voice in the trees shouted, 'Don't move.' The men came out of the bush, holding someone tightly by the arms. It was Joe.

Patrick looked at the young man, furious. He didn't want any more problems. 'Who is this?'

'I work at Tarong. I wasn't doing anything,' said Joe.

Berjenka took out a gun and pointed it at Joe. 'This has gone far enough – ' he began.

'No, wait. Maybe he's up to something,' said Patrick. 'Bring him here.'

Petersen punched Joe hard in the mouth. Joe fell to the ground, groaning. There was blood on his face.

'What were you doing?' Petersen demanded.

'Nothing,' Joe said weakly. 'I was just curious.'

'This is not good,' said Berjenka. 'Mr Forsha, you are not a careful man. We have to get out of here.'

Patrick picked Joe up from the ground and shouted in his face, 'Who else is with you?'

'No one. I said I was just curious.'

Patrick took a gun from his pocket and pointed it at

Joe's face. Judy was shocked. Now she knew Patrick was a monster.

There was a sound from the sky. They all looked up. Two planes had suddenly appeared over the top of the hill. The people on the ground could easily see markings under the wings. They belonged to the Australian air force.

'What is this, Forsha? You've led us into a trap!' said Berjenka.

Patrick let Joe fall on the ground. 'I know nothing about this,' he shouted. 'I'm getting out of here.'

He looked around, waving his gun wildly, then he grabbed Judy.

'You're coming with me.' He dragged her towards his helicopter. Petersen and his pilot were already climbing into the other one.

'Where do you think you are going?' shouted Berjenka, taking a gun from his pocket. Patrick turned round and fired. Berjenka fell to the ground. Blood poured from his arm.

Patrick pulled Judy into the helicopter. The engine was still going. She looked back. Joe was trying to get up, his face covered in blood. The other helicopter wasn't moving. The pilot was having problems starting it. Patrick's eyes were wild now.

'I'm sorry Judy. I don't want to hurt you, but –' he waved his gun, ' – you have to come with me.'

Now Petersen was running towards them, shouting, 'Let us on! Our helicopter's damaged! You can't leave us here!' Patrick raised his gun and fired again. Petersen dropped to the ground, holding his chest.

Judy screamed. Patrick didn't care about killing even his

own men! Patrick's helicopter was lifting off the ground. She had to do something. She saw Patrick had both hands on the controls, and then she remembered that Paul had told her that helicopter pilots needed two hands to take off and land.

She felt in her pocket for the perfume. She took it from her pocket and pushed the top down hard. A jet of perfume went directly into Patrick's eyes. He screamed and rubbed his eyes with one of his hands. He lost control of the helicopter, and it started to go round in circles. Judy grabbed the door handle, threw the door open and jumped out. She rolled on the ground, trying to get away from the helicopter. She got up and started running towards Joe. Patrick was starting to get control again. He turned the machine round, trying to get away.

Above the noise of the engine, shots could be heard. Holes appeared in the side of the helicopter. It hung in the air for a few seconds, then suddenly it was a ball of fire. Judy threw herself on the ground and hid her face. The next thing she remembered was men picking her up. Murri faces, she thought, all except one, a white man. He was holding a gun in one hand. His right leg was tied to a piece of wood.

'Are you OK, Judy?' said the white man.

'Dad!' Judy shouted.

Chapter 19 *Recovery*

The truck headed slowly back towards the farm. Joe's brother drove, while Joe and Judy sat in the back. Joe's nose was bleeding. An air force helicopter had picked up Judy's father and the other men.

'I still don't understand, Joe,' said Judy. 'I thought Dad was dead. We saw him at the bottom of the valley.'

'You saw a dummy,' said Joe. 'You remember the clothes I took from John's cupboard? We found your dad holding onto the edge of the rock. A few minutes later and he would have fallen off. We made a dummy with leaves and bits of wood, anything we could find. We put his clothes on it and gave him the others, and then we threw the dummy down to the bottom of the valley. We hoped those guys wouldn't get close enough to see. If they thought your dad was dead, they wouldn't worry about him any more.'

'It worked. I believed it,' she said, remembering the horror she had felt. 'What were you doing at the helicopter, Joe?'

'When I left you last night, we couldn't get in touch with the authorities. The truck radio was broken – just when we needed it. We couldn't fix it, so my ma took a car and drove through the night to the nearest town to call for help. We had to find a way to keep those guys from getting away until the authorities got here. So I took that horse you found and rode it here. We had some sugar at home. If you put sugar in an engine, it doesn't work. I thought that would keep them on the ground till help came. But, as you saw, they got me before I could get to the other guy's helicopter. I wonder who he was.'

'He . . . My mother knew him. I still can't believe it,' Judy said. She thought to herself, 'But now I understand. Patrick wanted to kill Dad so he could marry Mum.' She shook at the thought.

It was late afternoon when the truck stopped outside the farmhouse at Tarong. John Fittock came out to meet them with a Murri woman.

'What have they done to you?' said the woman, rushing towards Joe.

'This is my ma, Celia,' Joe explained to Judy. He turned to his mother. 'I'm OK, Ma, really.'

'Come inside,' said John. 'And we'll fix up your face, Joe.'

* * *

It was dark when Don woke up. He was lying on a soft bed. A woman was putting a warm towel on his face. He tried to get up.

'Judy . . .'

'I'm a nurse, Mr Radcliffe,' the woman said. 'You're in hospital. You passed out in the helicopter. I'm hardly surprised after all your adventures.'

'Where's my daughter? Is she OK?' Don asked.

'She'll be coming in to see you later. I believe she's had quite an adventure too.'

'I had no idea there would be any danger,' Don said quietly. 'I hadn't seen her for so long. I wanted to make up for lost time.'

'Family's the most important thing anyone's got,' the nurse said. 'I'm a Murri, and our people know that more than anyone. In the past we've been separated from our families by force. But you chose to go away. I don't understand you people.'

'You're right,' said Don. 'I've been stupid.'

'Anyway, you're awake. There's someone here who wants to speak to you.' The nurse left the room. A few moments later, a tall man came into the room. He came up to the bed and held out his hand.

'Mr Radcliffe? Noel Hogan,' he said. He took out a card and showed it to Don. It said Hogan was a government agent. 'Just a couple of questions. I expect you've got some, too.'

'I'm ready,' said Don.

'Did you know you were picking up uranium at Warrangi?'

'No, not at all,' Don replied. He told Hogan how the job with Paul had come about, and how they thought they were doing it for the government.

'It seems Forsha had paid people at the mine to keep quiet. The owner had certainly been bribed. We're arresting them all. You were really lucky, you know. No one would have found you, as the flight plan we checked had nothing about the mine on it. But fortunately, Judy's mother saw her at Warrangi on TV, on the day of the demonstration. And that's how we found you. Did you know Patrick Forsha?'

'I'd met him twice for a few minutes. He was seeing my ex-wife,' Don said.

'So you had no idea he was mixed up in all of this?'

Hogan said.

'Not at all,' Don replied. 'When I first saw his helicopter, I thought he'd come to rescue Judy.'

'So you had no idea about his business problems?' Hogan asked.

'Business problems?' Don said, surprised. 'I thought he had a lot of money.'

'He was in big trouble. He'd borrowed too much to put into his building company,' Hogan explained. 'His business was about to fail. Selling uranium to a foreign country was a way of bringing in a few million dollars. And hiring you to fly the plane was a way of getting you out of the way at the same time.'

Don looked shocked and angry.

'Who was he selling it to?'

'We can't say. The government wants to keep it quiet. It's somewhere in Asia, but their embassy says they know nothing about it. They're lying, of course.'

'What will happen to them?' Don asked.

Hogan sighed. 'Nothing. We can't touch embassies of foreign countries. We can only send some of their people home with a warning. At least Forsha didn't get away, thanks to you. A good shot, we hear.'

'He was trying to take Judy with him,' Don said.

'We know. It's OK. We won't be taking this any further.'

'What happens now?' asked Don.

'We'll take you back to Canberra with us. We may need a written statement from you about what happened.'

'Are we going now?'

'Soon. You have some visitors first.' He smiled, and opened the door. Sylvia and Judy came into the room. Judy had a newspaper under her arm.

'How are you doing, Dad?' Judy smiled.

'I'll be going,' said Hogan. He left the room, nodding to Sylvia.

'Look at this, Dad. Today's paper,' Judy said, opening the newspaper out and spreading it on the bed in front of him. The headline read, 'Mine Closes. Warrangi People Given Land Rights'. On the same page there was a picture of the *Sugar Glider* at Everett's Field, with the heading 'Pilot Found Alive'. The article said the crash had been an accident. There was nothing about uranium, Forsha or foreign governments.

'Don, I'm so glad you're all right. I still can't believe all of this . . . and Paul. It's terrible,' said Sylvia. She looked down. 'I nearly lost both of you.'

'It was lucky you saw Judy on TV,' Don replied.

The room fell silent as they all thought about what could have happened to their family.

'I'm sorry, Sylvia,' Don said.

'About what?'

'About everything. It shouldn't have happened.'

Sylvia touched his hand softly. 'We're coming to Canberra with you. When the authorities have finished with you, maybe you'd like to – '

'We want you to stay at the farm!' Judy interrupted.

'Is that OK, Sylvia?' Don looked into her eyes.

'Well, you can't fly for a while, can you?' She smiled.

'Then I think I'd like that very much,' Don said.

'Welcome home, Dad,' Judy said, and leaned over to kiss him.